MW01122247

21 Days to *Better* Family Entertainment

Books in the 21-Day Series

A Proven Plan
for Beginning
New Habits

21 Days to *Better* Family Entertainment

Robert G. DeMoss Jr.

Series Editor Dan Benson

ZondervanPublishingHouse
Grand Rapids, Michigan

A Division of HarperCollinsPublishers

21 Days to Better Family Entertainment
Copyright ©1998 Robert G. DeMoss Jr.

Requests for information should be addressed to:

ZondervanPublishingHouse
Grand Rapids, Michigan 49530

ISBN: 0-310-21746-6

Published in association with the literary agency of Alive Communications, Inc., 1465 Kelly Johnson Blvd., Suite 320, Colorado Springs, CO 80920

Interior design by Sherri Hoffman

Printed in the United States of America

98 99 00 01 02 03 04 /❖ DC/ 10 9 8 7 6 5 4 3 2 1

To Dave and Annette Weyerhaeuser,
For Your Steadfast Partnership and Faithful Support
to Reach America's Young People

CONTENTS

The Third Week: Taking On Other Contenders

INTRODUCTION

Is the music in your home a source of constant debate? Are you weary of the way television endlessly challenges your family's values while it spews profanity in prime time? Are you tired of sitting on the sidelines while today's popular entertainment mocks what is important to your family? Has your family forgotten how to play games, talk, or even take walks together?

If you answered yes to any of those questions, this book is *exactly* what you need!

Allow me to welcome you to the most exhilarating fight of your life: the battle to pick the best entertainment for your family. But be forewarned: don't read these pages unless you are mad. I mean seriously, knock-down, fighting mad. Why? Because I'm looking for people who want to become victorious in this arena—and winners are not made of indecisive dreamers.

"Whoa, Bob. Sounds a bit tough!"

You bet. Considering that what you're facing is a combined 20-*billion*-dollar music, film, and media industry, nothing short of a vigorous, no-nonsense approach will work. In the following pages, I provide you with a 21-day plan to maximize the entertainment choices your family makes. I'll be at your side every step of the way. My hunch is you'll actually come to enjoy our daily sessions and practical pointers. After all, I'll be drawing upon fifteen years of experience in this field of study.

I've had the opportunity to debate explicit entertainment on the *Phil Donahue Show, Geraldo, Good Morning America, National Public Radio,* and hundreds of radio and television stations across North America. As a former disc jockey, I can offer a perspective from behind the microphone. And having served seven years as the youth culture specialist for Dr. James Dobson and Focus on the Family, I've had the privilege of speaking to thousands of families in more than two hundred cities. Along the way, my research has received the thumbs up from Ann Landers, *Readers' Digest,* and ABC's *20/20.*

It will be a joy to share with you the concepts and tools I've gleaned over the years. When we're done you'll find your children will be more imaginative, they'll grow into avid readers, your spouse may actually become a more interesting and inquisitive conversationalist, and your family will draw closer to one another. Best of all, this book can help your young people reduce their inclination toward destructive juvenile choices in the process.

Hard to believe? Actually, if I'm guilty of anything it's that I may be *understating* the benefits of this book. Ready to get started? Great.

Since I'll be taking you through some practical application activities in each chapter, there are several things you'll need in order to squeeze the most out of this resource. Don't laugh at my list. Everything will make sense in due course. My guess is you'll have a number of these supplies around the house. Thankfully, they're all low cost items:

- A dozen yellow legal pads
- A clipboard for each family member
- A small penlight-type flashlight for each person
- Several poster boards
- A black permanent "sharpie" marker

- A mason jar (with lid) for each child in your home
- Several dozen 4" x 6" index cards
- Occasional copier access (public library, office, Kinko's)

In case you're having any second thoughts, here's one last word of encouragement. People frequently ask how I remain so optimistic after surveying the sickening state of today's entertainment landscape. After all, I've studied popular culture—and I've worked with teens and their families—for numerous years. Admittedly, there are times when it can get seriously overwhelming. But two things help me stay focused. The first is found in this playful poem:

Two frogs fell into a deep cream bowl,
  One was an optimistic soul.
The other took the gloomy view,
  We shall drown he cried, without more ado.
So with a last whooping cry,
  He flung up his legs and he said good-bye.
Said the other frog, with a merry grin,
  I can't get out, but I won't give in.
I'll just swim around, 'til my strength is spent,
  Then will I drown, the more content.
Bravely he swam, 'til it would seem,
  His struggles began, to churn the cream.
On top of the butter, at last he stopped,
  And out of the bowl, he gaily hopped!
What of the moral, 'tis easily found,
  If you can't hop out, keep swimming around!

I am unaware of the author, but the poet creatively reminds us we really have only two choices: either drown in our cultural depravity or work aggressively to overcome it.

The second resource that enables me to optimistically move forward is to remind myself of what God says in his Word. It's true some battles may be won by the opposition, and we might suffer short-term losses. *But*—the outcome of the war itself is already assured!

Jesus promised, "In this world you will have trouble. But take heart! I have overcome the world" (John 16:33). And, "Look, I am making all things new; these words are true and faithful" (Rev. 21:5). Likewise John the apostle, like a winning coach, assures us, "This is the victory that overcomes the world, even our faith" (1 John 5:4). In our fight for what is right, you and I can draw strength from the One who fought and overcame death itself! And it's through the strength of his might that we can confidently begin our study.

Is Hollywood the reigning heavyweight champ in your home? Don't worry. I have confidence that we *can* make a difference together. I'm ready if you are . . . so let's take it one day at a time!

THE FIRST WEEK

Taming the Tube

DAY 1

Breakfast of Champions?

Feeding Your Family Undivided Attention

Television has proved that people will look at any-thing rather than each other.

ANN LANDERS[1]

Before we get started, I'd like to introduce you to someone I've known for a number of years. He's quite an unusual character. He and I were close buddies a while back. Although I've sort of lost touch in recent times, I'd like to describe him. Just for fun, consider whether or not he'd be the kind of companion you'd enjoy spending time with in your home:

- He is well traveled and has a wealth of knowledge.
- He has an endless supply of interesting stories to share.
- His opinion is so important even the president seeks him.
- He's very effective as a teacher.
- He has a way with kids . . . they can't get enough of him!
- He loves a good time.
- He's sure to make you laugh.
- His gaze is irresistible.

- He's *very* popular and almost world famous.
- His style of communicating is simply mesmerizing.
- He's willing to spend as much time with you as you like.

In all fairness, he's far from a perfect person. Over the years, I've picked up on a number of annoying qualities. So, before you decide whether or not you'd like to meet him, let's consider the other side of his personality:

- He does *all* the talking and won't listen to your opinion.
- He's very demanding and requires your full attention.
- He's selfish and couldn't care less about your feelings.
- He doesn't share your Christian point of view.
- He's literally deaf and can't hear what you're saying.
- He'll present you with morally objectionable ideas.
- He rarely cautions you of the consequences of his advice.
- He frequently uses profanity.
- He's obsessed with sex.
- He has a habit of interrupting himself without warning.
- He can be unruly and at times difficult to control.
- He gravitates toward guns and enjoys explosives.
- Given enough time with you, he can be a bad influence.
- He's the kind of friend who is always putting things down, which tends to make you unhappy with the clothes you wear, the car you drive, the furniture you own, and even the moral choices you've made.

What do you think? Does this sound like a desirable individual to you? Can you picture yourself inviting him over for tea? Does he have the qualities you look for in a dinner guest? Would you have any problem allowing him to play with your children? Or to the contrary, does he resemble a nightmare you'd want to avoid at all costs?

The truth is, if your home is anything like 98% of households in North America, he's *already* comfortably ensconced in your kitchen, living room—maybe even in your bedroom. If you haven't guessed by now, my "friend" is the television set. Hard to believe? Go ahead. Reread the list of his characteristics. Compare them to your experience with the box and see if what I've described is true. After all, those are the very reasons why he and I are not so close these days!

Given the pivotal role television plays in our homes, we'll be spending the first full week of our 21-day plan examining this powerful medium, how it feeds the mind and how it shapes the souls of our loved ones. In fact, today your goal is to learn how to prevent your family from relying upon the electronic junk food TV serves at breakfast. And we'll do that by applying the next two practical exercises.

OATMEAL, OVALTINE, AND AN OBSERVATION

Cereal companies love to advertise the fact that their candy-coated, sugar-injected product is somehow "an important part" of a "nutritionally balanced diet." But skeptical parents scour grocery shelves for more appropriate choices. At the heart of this concern is the adage: "You are what you eat." Whether you settle on oatmeal or Ovaltine, I imagine you work hard to provide the family with healthy sustenance.

Now, be honest. Do you prepare and serve breakfast with the television on? Maybe you don't have one of those newfangled "space-saver" tubes available in one of "five designer real simulated plastic vinyl colors" perched on the windowsill. But is there a TV set percolating somewhere in the house while the family faces a new day?

If so, as of today make a decision to change the habit of watching *any* TV before, during, or immediately after breakfast. That means for you, your spouse, and the kids. (After all, if you're so concerned about the food your family eats, why pay such little attention to the media diet they ingest?)

You may be wondering, "But how? Won't they be fed up with me?" Not if your approach is properly handled. I'd begin by privately gaining the support of your better half for the idea. Then, before the rest of the family gets up, physically unplug all of the TV sets around the house. Next, bring a tape or CD player to the kitchen area and pick a favorite music selection to have playing in the background.

As the children come to the table, if they're in the habit of turning on the tube, they'll be surprised when it doesn't work. Use the occasion to explain that you'd like to try something different at breakfast for several days—no TV. With the older kids, let them know that you value a chance to talk with them and especially to listen to their plans for the day. If they seem paralyzed at how to respond or lack something to say—don't worry. They're just out of practice. Give them time.

With younger children, use the food metaphor. Explain that "we want to be more careful with the ideas we put into our minds." Just as we care to serve them food that's fresh and good for their growing bodies, we want to make better TV choices. And what about the spouse who depends upon CNN, ESPN, or other news networks for the morning headlines? Consider using either a newspaper or an all-news format radio station instead. I'm confident you'll find they hardly miss TV news after a handful of days. Best of all, you will have set the stage for improved family conversation instead of TV consternation.

MIND GAMES

Now that you've neutralized the nuisance of TV's morning breath, later in the week play this guessing game with your family. If you have a portable TV, place it on the center of the kitchen table. As they're eating, ask: "When you watch TV and see a program or a commercial message, what's missing from your encounter?" In other words, when compared to how they experience life, what's different about the way they relate to that electronic gadget? See how many things they can identify.

Need some help?

How about smell? Come to think of it, everything we see on TV lacks an aroma. That means we viewers cannot use our sense of smell to verify what we see. Do those delicious looking cinnamon rolls really smell as good as they look? You'll never know unless you go and buy one.

What about taste? Or touch? When we watch TV, we disengage our ability to confirm the claims of an advertisement through rather fundamental means. Is that toilet paper really "soft as a cloud"? Are those French fries really hot and crisp? Even our seeing mechanisms are hampered because the images are often delivered in quick video cuts, which don't allow for careful consideration. Or the close-up shots make objects look larger-than-life. Likewise, people are presented in favorable lighting and special make-up that masks flaws.

Digging deeper, also missing from the television experience is *interaction* and *dialogue*. Help your kids see how it's only a one-sided conversation, one where TV does all of the talking and never listens to our opinion. Nor does it care about it.

While you're quizzing those inquisitive minds, don't lose sight of the big picture. Use their answers and insights to move toward today's goal: preventing your family from relying upon the electronic junk food TV serves at breakfast. I'd contend that the best defense is a strong offense. If you can get them to question how television feeds their mind, you've opened the doorway to future success!

Inclined Recliner

Counting the Real Cost of TV Consumption

Television has opened many doors—mostly on refrigerators.

MARY H. WALDRIP[1]

Have you ever experienced a tornado? Watching a movie like the box office hit *Twister* was enough to convince me I wouldn't want to be in the same state as one. Somehow funnel-shaped clouds traveling at upwards of 500 miles an hour while trashing everything in its path isn't my idea of a good time.

But shortly after my family and I relocated to Nashville, Tennessee, guess what? A rather feisty tornado touched down a mere 30 miles from our new home. Talk about a welcoming committee. Watching the news accounts the following morning, I found myself laughing uncontrollably—not at the devastation, mind you. More than 200 homes and businesses were damaged or demolished during this tragedy. What set me into a fit of laughter was a small detail in one news account.

You see, the network affiliates sent the camera crews to speak with a number of the victims.

They interviewed one woman who spent several minutes recalling the terror of the winds blasting out her windows. She spoke of furniture flying crazily through the house—just like a scene out of Dorothy's experience in the *Wizard of Oz*. She explained how she ran from her home and crossed the street to safety at the house of a neighbor who had a basement.

Here's the detail that sent me spinning.

As this lady's entire house collapsed behind her, she fled clutching one prized possession: her television remote control! I'm absolutely serious. Not a piece of the family china. No apparent second thoughts about the pet. Not even the family Bible. No. Her one and only possession rescued that day was her silly TV remote control.

BLOWN AWAY

How about you? On a given night, if you were suddenly driven out of your house, what might be in your hand? If you're like the overwhelming majority of Americans, it may very well be that crazy remote control. Why? Because the average family in this country views about 7 hours of TV *per day*.

Take a minute to calculate the mathematical implications of this over a lifetime using less than *half* of the national average. At 3 hours a day multiplied by 365 days, you'd watch 1,095 hours in one year. Viewing 1,095 hours per year over 60 years you'd log a whopping 65,700 hours. That's the equivalent of more than 7 *years* of watching the tube *24 hours per day*—whew!

What's more, syndicated columnist Don Feder found that 66% of families regularly watch television while eating dinner. Mathematically speaking, the odds that you might be embracing the TV clicker are relatively high.

Is it difficult to believe that your television plays such a central part in your family life? Do you honestly believe you don't have a significant financial investment in the TV? Stay tuned. Today we'll do something of paramount importance: gain a realistic picture of how much your family relies on the box. This analysis provides us with a *benchmark* for your future improvement. With this benchmark, after your family works through this book and begins to implement a number of the ideas, you'll be able to look back at how far you've actually come!

For instance, if you've ever gone swimming in the ocean you've probably experienced the sensation of drifting down the coast. Although it doesn't feel like you've traveled far, one glance at the location of your beach chairs reveals you've actually journeyed a surprising distance. Without a benchmark, it's difficult to discern your movement.

The same is true at a weight-loss center. When you first enroll in a program, they weigh you *and* make a note of your various body measurements. Some go so far as to photograph you—which feels especially embarrassing when the would-be dieter already feels like the Goodyear blimp. Yet this provides a picture of the starting point. It's not particularly pleasant at the time, but looking back it becomes a source of great encouragement.

So in the name of documenting your progress, let's measure 2 things. First, *time consumption*. Second, *financial considerations*. Brace yourself. The results of our exercise in the next section may come as a surprise.

GET DISCONNECTED

Today, let's get down to business. I'd like for you to create a television viewing log. It's not complicated. All you need is a clipboard, a pen or pencil, and several sheets of lined notebook paper. Now, write across the top something like "The DeMoss Family TV Log"—inserting your family's name, of course. Then, make 5 columns, placing these headings at the top: "Date," "Name," "Program Watched," "Video," and "Length of Program."

Now place the clipboard by the television set. (If you have several TVs around the house, it's important to put a log at each location for more accurate results). At breakfast or dinner explain to the family that you're conducting a test. Show them the log and demonstrate how to fill it out. It's fairly self-explanatory.

After writing in the date, the name or names of the person(s) watching, along with the show selected, simply write in the length of time spent viewing the tube. If it's a video that's being watched, have them place a check mark in the "Video" column. If the program is nothing more than flipping across the dial, write "Channel surfing" in the "Program Watched" column. Do this for seven days, then add up the amount of time spent watching TV. Make sure to include ALL viewing—sports, news, movies, soaps, cartoons, and specials.

To help the family hold one another accountable, consider offering a 25¢ reward if you catch someone watching the TV without filling in the log *before* they begin to watch. The reward can be an amount more or less than what I've suggested. The key is to make it age appropriate.

If you have young people who don't want to participate because they think it's a "stupid" idea, take them aside and gently tell them you really need their support. Encourage them to be a leader in the family. If that doesn't motivate them, consider withholding a treat (such as dessert) or deprive them of a privilege (Internet access, going to the mall) until they come on board. Single parents or those who have latchkey kids may have to operate on the honor system.

Add up your one week test; write the total here: _____ .

To monitor your progress, retake the test 3 weeks after completing this book and compare how your family did. My hunch is you'll notice a significant decrease in TV watching.

THE PRICE IS RIGHT?

As our preceding activity will ultimately demonstrate, we spend a significant amount of *time* in front of the box. But have you ever calculated how much cash you're investing to watch television? Let's take a look at how much money it actually costs an average family to watch the TV. (After my sample, why not recalculate it using your family's figures.)

First, we'll use an average purchase price for buying a VCR and television. The life expectancy of these units are roughly 5 years and 10 years respectively. In the far right column you'll notice I've amortized the cost of buying a VCR and TV set over its life span in order to arrive at an *annual expense* to own them.

Annual Financial Costs of Television Viewing

SAMPLE

Average monthly cable/satellite bill = $26

Multiply that figure by 12 months:	$312
Cost of VCR = $375 divided by a 5-year lifespan:	$ 75
Number of TVs = 3	
Estimated cost of those sets: $1,200 divided by a 10-year lifespan:	$120
15 videos purchased	$285
40 videos rented per year	$ 80
Estimated electricity to power VCR & TVs per year Based upon $10 per month:	$120
Purchase of special chairs (such as a recliner) to enhance viewing. Cost $500 spread over 10 years:	$ 50
TOTAL EXPENSE TO WATCH TV PER YEAR:	$1,042

By way of perspective, a couple earning $30,000 per year is spending 1/30th of their annual income just to participate in this *optional* activity! But wait, there's more ... you'll notice I didn't factor in the added expense of "TV munchies" consumed while watching television. All of those chips, microwave popcorn bags, pretzels, and sodas over the course of one year probably add another $250–$300 to the annual expense picture.

These two expenditures—*time consumption* and *financial considerations*—lead us to the heart of the matter: What are you receiving for this investment? Is your family really better off because of the time and money spent to experience the artificial world of TV-land? In other words, are you getting your money's worth?

Based upon my personal experience, I can attest to the fact that there is a richer, fuller experience awaiting your family if, and when, you reduce your dependency on this national pastime. If you desire to make that change but don't know how to unhook your lovable—but TV dependent—family, be encouraged! We'll tackle specific ideas tomorrow.

When Pay TV Pays Off

Reinforcing Participation in Real-Life Activities

Children will watch anything, and when a broadcaster uses crime and violence and other shoddy devices to monopolize a child's attention it's worse than taking candy from a baby. It is taking precious time from the process of growing up.

NEWTON MINOW[1]

Have you ever visited a friend's house for coffee and a little intimate conversation, only to find yourself competing for attention with their TV set? How did it make you feel? Somewhat neglected? Relatively unimportant? And what about the dynamic at your house? Does your own television set dominate the family dynamic? Do your children value watching TV over other more valuable activities? I know how you feel.

It's amazing the place of prominence our society affords the tube. Although we can't change the rest of society (or an inconsiderate host who invites us to tea only to watch TV) we *can* reset *our* family's priorities. How? By taking control of *time management* of the tube, which is today's goal.

FROM THE HEART

I remember one day when my wife, Leticia, came home from a women's fellowship group. That particular luncheon, the women spent the majority of time comparing notes about their problem child: the TV. By the sounds of it, TV must have been public enemy #1. Have a listen.

Linda, a mother of three sitting on Leticia's left, exclaimed, "My husband and I are so sick of the trash on television we're ready to put the box in the garage for at least a month—maybe longer! We're fed up."

Caroline confessed in utter frustration, "I'll admit that I use the TV as a baby-sitter. But how else can I get a few minutes alone?"

Equally honest was Susan, who owned up to the fact that "When I come home, I'm beat. Is it wrong to desire a few hours of mindless humor? Frankly, I need the escape after my day at the office." Have you ever felt like that?

Then there was Nicole who worked afternoons as a nanny. She reached the end of her wits because "even though I provide games, art supplies, even models to work on, the children come home and immediately race for the television. I'm not sure why I even bother to create alternatives—they just don't have an interest." I understand that feeling! We've been down that road in our house many times.

Much could be said about each of their frustrations. For instance, Susan's situation says something about her choice of job. I find it difficult to believe that an escape is required *every* evening. If things are that stressful at the office, perhaps it's time to look for a healthier work environment rather than attempting to pacify the pain by staring at the cold flickering light of the boob tube. There are numerous ways to relax besides that choice.

Nicole's comment is precisely where I'd like to begin today's study. I want to address a simple but effective way to enable our younger children (ages 4 to 11) to get into the habit of *participating* in life—rather than passively consuming TV's radiation. Nicole's observation, that "they just don't have an interest" is where we'll start.

Your first goal will be to make television *less interesting* by causing it to *offer fewer choices*. How? Let's look at 3 easy steps.

STEP 1: PULL THE PLUG

If you have cable or satellite service, begin by canceling your service today. Do it *now*—*before* second thoughts weaken your will. (Don't worry. You can always resubscribe. I'm confident your cable company will gladly resume taking your hard-earned cash every month.) By pulling the plug on pay TV, you'll accomplish 2 things. First, you send a signal to the family that you mean business—you're ready to put that box in its place.

Secondly, you'll benefit by saving money on cable (or satellite) fees. In some instances those savings are substantial—as much as between $25 and $49 a month. As you'll discover tomorrow, we'll use a portion of these savings to help our young people learn how to cherish more important activities.

STEP 2: BROADCAST THE NEWS

Over dinner, have this conversation with the family. "Kids, your father [or mother as the case may be] and I have a very important decision to discuss as a family. We've noticed that all of us are guilty of spending far too much time with the TV. We've also found that too many of the programs on television contain ideas, words, and actions of which we don't approve." (You may begin to notice a few drops of sweat beading on some foreheads—this is normal.)

You might detail a few specifics of your concern. For instance, mention a show that regularly depicts kids sassing their parents. Or, as is sadly the case in many prime time shows, programs that use profanity in the dialogue or use the Lord's name in vain. As you describe these offensive elements, remember to explain you're concerned that your family may begin to emulate the attitudes and language that TV's fantasy world posits as normal.

"That's why today we will be calling the cable company to cancel our service. We'd still be able to receive the basic broadcasting channels—and we can make use of the video player—but for now those will be our only TV options. That's right—no more *Nick at Night* or Cartoon Network."

Again, the goal here is to reduce the perceived value of scanning the dial. At this juncture, it's important to ask them, "What are your feelings about this change?" Allow them to express what's going on in their minds.

In some cases, such as with older siblings, it might be a good idea to solicit the children's input before removing the cable. Ask them what they think about the issues and concerns you've identified. I raise this point for those parents who might already be perceived as the family dictator. We don't want to fuel that notion! By inviting input, we share authority and responsibility with them. Which, in turn, helps to make them an ally rather than an adversary.

STEP 3: EXPLAIN THE PLAN

When it comes to viewing TV, one of the most difficult challenges to counter is the matter of *perceived value*. On the surface, TV's colorful, fast-paced images are mesmerizing. To a child, the loud music, action, and elements of fun are perceived as being enjoyable. But after viewing hour upon hour of TV, what do young people really have to show for his time? Very little. No words of affirmation or praise. No sense of accomplishment. No certificate of adulation.

How do you address this matter of perceived value? I'd suggest giving praise and awards for things children create, games they play, or books they read. Children who only watch TV will find out quickly that they are *never* rewarded for that activity. Today, you'll explain to the children that they now have a choice. They're permitted to watch an hour or so of television. Or they can draw a colorful picture, build something with the Legos, form an object from clay, read a book, or play a game.

Then, if they behave appropriately during those activities, they will be awarded stars according to this chart:

Award Level	Activity
No stars:	Watching TV or playing video games
1 star:	Playing a game, making a puzzle
2 stars:	Drawing, modeling, creating
3 stars:	Reading, helping with extra chores
4 stars:	Bible verse memorization

Here's where you hook them: Twice each week, announce that the person who accumulates the most stars will be the one who draws a prize from the prize hat! Make a game out of it. Let them have an idea of what they could win. One variation would be to consider making everyone a winner. The person with the most stars draws from the hat first, and so on. If you choose this option, it's a good idea to have a minimum of 10 stars to be able to pick a prize.

Speaking of prizes, I imagine you may be wondering where you'll come up with enough creative ideas to ensure their participation. Don't worry. That's the focus of our time together tomorrow. Meanwhile, if you still haven't done it, why not place that call to the cable company. You'll be glad you did!

Door Prizes, Jackpots, and Gifts Galore!

A Rewarding Incentive Plan

*There is more treasure in books than in all the pirates'
loot on* Treasure Island *... and best of all, you can
enjoy these riches every day of your life.*

WALT DISNEY[1]

Isn't it interesting that Walt Disney, a man who spent a lifetime creating movies and specials for television, still placed a higher premium on the activity of *reading!* That's why yesterday we explored ways to encourage *participation* in real-life activities such as reading, drawing, and creating figures from Legos or clay. The key is to make television *less attractive.* We decided one of the best ways to help children become unglued from the tube was to provide an incentive plan.

I'm sure the thought may have crossed your mind: "But Bob, where am I going to get all of the jackpot money?" That's a fair concern. Don't forget the money you'll save now that you've called the cable company and requested to be disconnected. But as you'll see in a moment, the gifts don't always have to involve cash. So, let's take a minute to write each of the following prizes onto separate pieces of paper (measuring 2" by 2") or on 3" x 5" index cards. Then place them in a hat, buckets or gift box. At the appropriate time, you'll invite your twice-weekly winners to reach in and draw their prize.

Remember, this is only a partial list of possible rewards. Get creative and have fun with it. And from time to time mix them up with new ideas as you think of them. As a matter of fact, why not invite the family to suggest ideas for prizes they'd enjoy earning too! Incidentally, the suggestions below are primarily for a younger set. If you have teens, get their input—I'm sure they'll have no problem coming up with a list of desirable rewards!

• **Staying up late on Friday night**

As adults, we forget what a big deal it is to be permitted to stay up later than your brothers or sisters. Granting an extra hour or so to play, read, or just visit with you is a real thrill. Friday night is best because it's not a school night, and unlike Saturday night, they won't be tired for church Sunday morning.

• **A healthy treat**

I've heard many nutritionists warn of the danger of rewarding good behavior with junk food (cakes, cookies, ice cream, *et al.*). Far be it from me to suggest even the occasional use of such items. Look for a quasi-healthy treat such as a caramel apple or nonfat caramel popcorn.

• **Breakfast in bed**

Find a baking sheet. Place a brightly-colored dish towel over it—instant breakfast tray! Your honored child will love this special treatment. One word of caution we learned from experience: Avoid serving a meal that involves syrup, blueberries, or glasses filled with too much liquid in them!

• **Getting an extra-special bedtime story**

Even at 10 years of age, my daughter Carissa absolutely loves it when I read to her at bedtime. This reward enables the child to request a bonus story any 3 nights of the following week.

• **"Take me out to the ball game"**

I have incredible memories of the times my father took me to see the Philadelphia Phillies back at the old Connie Mack Stadium. This prize may stretch your wallet a little, but you might offer 2 tickets to see a ball game—1 for the winner, and 1 for a friend of his choosing. Of course, you'll be along for the drive. (As a variation you could offer just one ticket). In some areas, there are wonderful minor league games or even the high school or local college football game that provide a more affordable option.

• **Golden plate award**

Here is a prize that lasts all week long. Find a specially-colored or uniquely-shaped dinner dish. The person who wins this will be served all dinner meals on this plate for the next week, signifying their accomplishment the previous week.

• **Swimming "date" to the YMCA**

If you're a member of the "Y" or similar club, this provides you with the perfect opportunity for some special one-on-one time. Saturday mornings are a great time for this award.

• **Exclusive arcade action**

Family fun centers are springing up all across the country. It's amazing how much fun my daughter and I have on the mini-golf course. Sometimes, as a special treat, I'll give her $5 in tokens and let her play whatever arcade game her little heart desires. Half of the fun is when she gets to turn in the tickets she's won for various trinkets behind the counter.

• **Quarters for TV quitters**

The kids who win obviously had to quit watching some level of TV in order to secure their stars. This award provides a quarter for each star they earned. As an alternative, use a dime or nickel depending on your budget and their age.

• **Low cost prizes**

There are a host of items that cost under 2 bucks. Some of our favorites include: a Happy Meal, colorful stickers, special pencil or pen, and knickknack jewelry.

• **The Mr. Bubble royal treatment**

Bath times become extra special with this award. In addition to adding Mr. Bubble to the tub, use a cassette player to provide a little bathing listening pleasure. Allow your kids to pick a favorite music tape or select a drama series. As an added bonus, prepare a snack such as apple slices for them to munch on. (Be sure to keep the tape player far away from the water in the tub!)

• **Free chore pass**

Draft something along the lines of: "This Official Chore Buster Certificate entitles the bearer to skip any chore of their choosing. Valid for seven days after receipt." Indicate this can be used for either a normal chore or any special requests that may arise.

• **Mad money**

I'd recommend maybe a couple of dollars (depending on the age of the kids) which they are permitted to spend any way they choose.

• **Super sundae**

You can buy an ice cream sundae for less than a dollar at most fast food restaurants. I'd suggest that rather than using the drive-thru, go and sit together in a relaxed manner as you enjoy sharing a quiet moment with your proud winner.

• **Savings account deposit**

Unlike the mad money, you'll make a deposit of $3–$5 to a savings bank. You can determine with the child what the ultimate purpose of this account is, such as a bicycle, roller blades, perhaps a collectible doll.

After detailing the plan we discussed yesterday—including the fact that there will be opportunities to win prizes—unveil the official scoreboard. Using a piece of poster board, write each person's name down on the left side. Place stars as they are earned to the right of the name. Position the poster board in a central location (the side of the refrigerator, a kitchen bulletin board) so the whole family can follow their daily progress. There's no reason why you can't foster a little healthy competition.

There's one final move to sweeten the jackpot.

At the end of the month, tally up the weekly scores to determine the grand prize winner. This person can select *any* of the available prize options rather than draw from the prize hat. My hunch is that with time, you won't even need to offer awards for alternative activities. Once a child relearns how to enjoy participating in life, television truly loses its audience.

Two Ways to Watch What You Watch

Engaging the Mind Instead of the Recliner

I pride myself on the fact that my work has no socially redeeming value.

JOHN WATERS, FILMMAKER[1]

The other day an associate e-mailed me this interesting list of oxymorons: "exact estimate," "genuine imitation," "legally drunk," "pretty ugly," "passive aggression," "peace force," "simulated reality," "tight slacks," "rap music," "12-ounce pound cake," and "educational TV." Actually, I'd take issue with his last example.

As I'm sure you can tell by now, it's my opinion that *all* television is "educational." Any time the television is on, its programs transmit values, morals, ideologies, and attitudes about life. In my first book, *Learn to Discern*, I referred to this as "edutainment"—education wrapped neatly in the package of entertainment. And, yes, even seemingly innocent programs frequently express beliefs that differ widely from our value system.

Allow me one example.

I'm sure you've had the experience of viewing a nature show on PBS at one time or another. Whether diving deep beneath the ocean's surface to study the life-cycle of an octopus, or chasing an antelope in the wild, the camera catches unbelievable pictures of these marvels of God's creation. However, the announcer invariably makes a comment about the "millions of years" it took for these creatures to *evolve*. There you have it. In a passing moment, the assertion that the theory of evolution is a fact is quietly slipped into the narration. (Worse, without your clarification, it's possible the children will accept that statement as fact.)

It's easy to miss the reality that all television has educational implications. Even the president receives a failing grade on that point. On July 29, 1996, Bill Clinton brokered a deal between television executives and children's advocates mandating an increase in the number of hours of "educational programming" aired on the major networks. The deal called for a total of 3 hours of so-called "educational" TV per week which must be aired between 7:00 A.M. and 10:00 P.M. And it must have a stated goal of serving the intellectual or emotional needs of young viewers.

Although that sounds good on the surface, as we've discussed, TV is *already* educational. A more valuable step would be a national effort to teach kids *how to watch* TV and *how to understand* what is being taught. Wouldn't you agree?

Rather than wait for the government to catch a vision for media literacy, we'll make this our objective today.

THE MATCH GAME

Our first goal—to teach children *how to watch* TV—requires a little effort and creativity on our part. After all, they may have already acquired the bad habit of simply staring at the box while disengaging their minds. That's why our first step is to help them see what they're seeing. And, more importantly, to see what they're NOT seeing. Let me explain.

I've found that whenever possible the best way to teach is to make a game out of our instruction. I'm not sure where I first came across the following activity, but it's both fun and effective. It's designed primarily to enable young viewers to recognize the types of behaviors TV most frequently uses to entertain the audience.

Here's how the game works. Below are 2 lists of words describing a wide range of situations. A number of these actions are commonly found in today's television programming, while others are virtually absent from the screen. Your child's objective is to identify the action when they see it.

Word list for children 7 to 12

Explosion	A gun shot	A mean comment
Car chase	A villain	People doing good
Hugging a parent	Smoking	A police car
A murder	An act of love	A puppet
Soft drink ad	Someone crying	Food ad
Kissing	Stealing	People winning $$
Praying	People at church	Game show
A toy ad	Screaming	People dancing
A Bible	Hitting	A minister

Word list for older children 12 to 16

Premarital sex	Homosexual behavior
Adultery	Fidelity
Forgiveness	Act of compassion
Drug usage	Act of violence
Consequences of a bad choice	A clean joke
Offensive language	Parents as idiots
Anger	Drunkenness
Depression	Sex celebrated in marriage
A rock star	Kids as smarter than adults
Someone depressed	Unconditional love displayed

Depending on the age of your young people, provide them with the appropriate list of adjectives/actions along with a hand-drawn tick-tack-toe grid. Next, have them select any 9 actions from the list and write them in any of the nine spaces on the grid. For example:

Car chase	Kissing	Act of love
Explosion	Praying	Stealing
Villain	Gun shot	Hitting

As they watch television, have them put an X through the action when they see it. Three X's in any direction wins the game.

After playing the game several times, it may dawn on an observant child that the actions of praying, going to church, displays of unconditional love, kindness, and the like are rarely pictured. When that occurs, we've made progress helping them to see what they *don't* see on TV.

That's the perfect time to ask: Why do you think TV rarely portrays people loving unconditionally, kids hugging their parents, or people praying? Further, what might these shows be teaching us when they ignore such important aspects of life? That they're unimportant? That nobody does them? That doing such things are unpopular or uninteresting?

Keep in mind as the family goes to play this game, I'm not suggesting that any ol' program will do. Sorry. Certain shows with an offensive track record ought to be obviously out of bounds. Writer Frank Rich said it best in a *New York Times* editorial. He observed, "If adults were serious about eliminating coarse TV, they would turn off *Married . . . With Children* and refuse to subscribe to risqué cable channels. American children will never grow up in a healthier electronic environment unless their parents grow up first."[2]

So let's not use the excuse of "research" to justify a poor choice. Instead, when viewing any normal family show, that's the time to play this game.

ROVING REPORTER

The second way to teach youngsters *how to watch TV* and *understand* the messages TV teaches is to have them become a reporter. For example, at age 10 our daughter is permitted to watch only 30 minutes of television on a school night—provided her homework is completed. Recently, she came to me and asked if she could increase her viewing time to an hour. I was familiar with both shows she enjoys and felt this would be the perfect time to expand her understanding of TV.

I agreed with Carissa's request for additional time, provided that she take notes during both programs! Not wanting to be a total killjoy, I asked her to do 3 simple things whenever she watched a show:

1. Report what the show was about
2. Report what was enjoyable
3. Report any parts which she disliked, disagreed with, or which were wrong

To make the process easier, we provided her with a small pad in which to make her observations. Frankly, at first she was hesitant. But she agreed when I explained that if we're going to spend a whole hour every day doing something, it made sense to get the *most* out of it.

Then over dinner we made time for Carissa to give us her report. As parents, we should find it encouraging to hear our children apply their faith to the things they see on television. I've found that Carissa often feels more deeply about what is right and wrong than I do as her dad. Perhaps we adults have grown either too callous or too comfortable with the things in entertainment that should break our hearts.

Incidentally, do your best to really pay attention when your children file their report. If you have to put down your fork for a minute in order to focus on what they're saying, do it. Thanks to the wonders of a microwave you can always reheat your meal. But if you miss what they're saying, you could fail to see into the window of their souls.

Why is this important?

Imagine your children explaining that their favorite part of a program was the violence, the hyper-charged laser cannon, or the cool slow motion explosions. These should be GIANT clues that your youngsters may have a propensity towards aggression. Sadly, far too often we don't *listen* to them, making it easy to miss the early warning signs of behavior that we should be addressing.

In fact, here's a novel idea. After dinner instead of racing to be the first one in the recliner, why not lounge at the table. Dust off the Bible and locate a passage that speaks to the issues your childen have raised. (A topical Bible can be an awesome aid.) Allow the power of the Scriptures to nurture their discerning spirit. I believe you'll find that extra effort will enable their discernment skills to "kick-in" automatically—even when they're not playing the part of a reporter down the road.

Now *that's* an incredible scoop!

Your Secret Weapon

Fight Back—On Your Knees

Is prayer your steering wheel or your spare tire?
                                    CORRIE TEN BOOM[1]

How's your week going? Are you frustrated, attempting to "sell" these ideas to your family? I imagine you may feel like the guy who, reflecting on his inability to market an idea, commented, "I couldn't sell a bale of hay to a hungry bull!" Without a doubt it can be tough going at times.

That's why today we'll fine-tune your secret weapon: prayer. In fact, let's engage your entire family while we're at it. Let me suggest that you move to a comfortable work space such as a desk or the kitchen table. Locate 14 index cards (4" x 6") and a pen or fine point marker. (If you happen to have a portable typewriter or access to a word processor, that's a bonus—but not necessary.)

I've provided 14 scriptures and prayerful insights relating to various aspects of the world of entertainment. In just a minute, either type or handwrite that information onto the cards.

Tonight at dinner, have someone draw a card to read either before or after the meal. Each card contains a prayer focus, a verse of Scripture, and a prayer reflection dealing with one aspect of popular entertainment.

It's so simple, yet so powerful.

The 14 cards are enough for 2 full weeks. After you've exhausted your supply, invite the family to come up with another 7 cards. This will complete 21-days of a culture prayer focus. Who knows, maybe it'll become a tradition that your family incorporates. What's more, we're assured that "The prayer of a righteous man is powerful and effective" (James 5:16).

Let's get started making up those cards. On the top line write the subject heading I've proposed—that is, MUSIC, VIDEO GAMES, THE INTERNET. Next, rewrite the Scripture reference on the first several lines of the card. Below that write out the prayer reflection. Feel free to copy it verbatim or rewrite it in your own words. (These are in no particular order.)

• MUSIC

Ps. 40:3: "He put a new song in my mouth, a hymn of praise to our God. Many will see and fear and put their trust in the LORD."

Prayer Reflection: Dear Jesus, thank you for the gift of music. Listening to music makes our life so much more enjoyable. Help our family to be wise in the music choices we make. Amen.

• ENTERTAINMENT

Rom. 12:2: "And do not be conformed to this world, but be transformed by the renewing of your mind, that you may prove what the will of God is, that which is good and acceptable and perfect" [NAS].

Prayer Reflection: Dear Jesus, at times we feel pressure to watch and listen to what our friends are into. Help us to be different, to look for the *best* options, ones that please you. Amen.

• THE INTERNET

Phil. 4:8: "Finally, brothers, whatever is true, whatever is noble, whatever is right, whatever is pure, whatever is lovely, whatever is admirable—if anything is excellent or praiseworthy—think about such things."

Prayer Reflection: Dear Jesus, thank you for the gift of technology. But there are so many temptations on the Internet. Help me to seek out only the praiseworthy Net sites, and to be a good witness by my example—even in a chat room. Amen.

• VIDEO GAMES

Gen. 6:13: "So God said to Noah, 'I am going to put an end to all people, for the earth is filled with violence because of them. I am surely going to destroy both them and the earth.'"

Prayer Reflection: Dear Jesus, in the days of Noah you were so angry with all of the violence in the world that you sent the flood. Today, you're probably just as concerned about the violence in video games. So help us to find games that aren't violent and change my heart to desire a better way. Amen.

• TELEVISION

John 11:35: "Jesus wept."

Prayer Reflection: Dear Jesus, I don't ever want to be the reason why you cry. I don't want to break your heart like that. When I watch TV, give me wisdom to make choices that please you. Amen.

• MOVIES

Luke 11:34: "Your eye is the lamp of your body. When your eyes are good, your whole body also is full of light. But when they are bad, your body also is full of darkness."

Prayer Reflection: Dear Jesus, thank you for the gift of sight. Give us the wisdom to watch more carefully what we watch. We don't want our lives to be filled with the darkness of this world. Amen.

• MAGAZINES

Col. 3:2: "Set your minds on things above, not on earthly things."

Prayer Reflection: Dear Jesus, as we read magazines today, it's easy to see that many people who write the articles don't believe in you. Help us not to be manipulated by an ungodly perspective. Amen.

• MOVIES

Col. 3:5–6: "Put to death, therefore, whatever belongs to your earthly nature: sexual immorality, impurity, lust, evil desires and greed, which is idolatry. Because of these, the wrath of God is coming."

Prayer Reflection: Dear Jesus, it's fun to go to the movies. But when I watch a film or rent a video, help me to compare what I'm seeing to this list of sinful behaviors. If what I'm viewing displeases you, give me the courage to leave or turn it off. Amen.

• ENTERTAINMENT

Heb. 12:2: "Let us fix our eyes on Jesus, the author and perfecter of our faith, who for the joy set before him endured the cross, scorning its shame, and sat down at the right hand of the throne of God."

Prayer Reflection: Dear Jesus, sometimes kids at school mock me because I'm not allowed to watch certain shows or listen to certain tapes. But when the world mocked you, you resisted. Help me to have that same strength and courage to do the right thing. Amen.

• TELEVISION

Ps. 101:3: "I will set no worthless thing before my eyes; I hate the work of those who fall away; It shall not fasten its grip on me" (NAS).

Prayer Reflection: Dear Jesus, I must confess sometimes I get so lazy, I just sit in front of the television flipping through the channels. I pray that I'll be more careful not to settle on worth-less programming. Amen.

• MUSIC

Matt. 12:36–37: "But I tell you that men will have to give account on the day of judgment for every careless word they have spoken. For by your words you will be acquitted, and by your words you will be condemned."

Prayer Reflection: Dear Jesus, I love to sing along with today's music. And it sounds like you place a premium on proper speech. When I'm singing, help me to be selective with my choices. Amen.

• ENTERTAINMENT

1 John 1:9: "If we confess our sins, He is faithful and right-eous to forgive us our sins and to cleanse us from all unright-eousness" [NAS].

Prayer Reflection: Dear Jesus, I confess that it's not easy to always please you with the entertainment choices I make. For-give me when I get lazy, tired, or don't care enough to do what's right. Amen.

• TELEVISION

James 3:6: "The tongue also is a fire, a world of evil among the parts of the body. It corrupts the whole person, sets the whole course of his life on fire, and is itself set on fire by hell."

Prayer Reflection: Dear Jesus, when I see people on TV using angry or hateful words, I'm reminded of this verse. It's so true that my tongue can easily become corrupted. Help me to select shows where people are using their tongues responsibly. Amen.

• MUSIC

Ps. 146:2: "I will praise the LORD all my life; I will sing praise to my God as long as I live."

Prayer Reflection: Dear Jesus, thank you for inspiring Christians to make music for me to enjoy. It really helps me to grow in my faith. Help me to find good contemporary Christian alternatives to build a strong music collection. Amen.

Two final observations. It's possible some children may whine, "Why do we have to do this?" The response we use in our home is something along the lines of, "Because we're trying to raise the DeMoss family differently, to love Jesus with all of our hearts. We're responsible to God to guide you so when you're older, you'll know how to turn to God to make the right choices and decisions on your own." We've found the key is to smother them in love and kindness.

The second insight concerning these prayer cards is found in something my old college professor was fond of saying: The heart of the matter is a matter of the heart! The reason why my family uses these cards is because we don't want to break the heart of God. Since we have come to know him personally and have developed an intimate relationship with him, our desire is to please him—especially in the areas of personal entertainment choices.

That's why we frequently pray, "Lord, help me to love what you love, and hate what you hate." Will you join us in teaching your family that prayer?

DAY 7

Setting Standards When Settings Aren't Standard

Eight Insights to Strengthen Your Foresight

Films and TV shows have so much influence. They impart so much information that can define the expectation of what it means to be a man or a woman, of what's fun and what's not, of what's acceptable and what's not. So I'm very cautious about that with the kids.

SUSAN SARANDON[1]

Looking back over our first week together, I bet you might have had this thought: "Okay, Bob. These concepts are fine when we're at home with the kids. We can control their choices with minimal hassle. But what about all of the times they're not in this ideal setting?"

That's a fair question and I'm glad you asked.

I've received many wonderful suggestions pertaining to 8 unusual situations that are likely to happen sooner or later. I'm confident these ideas on how to set (and maintain) standards apart from your normal routine will come in handy down the road. At the same time, ask the Lord to keep your kids' moral compass working properly. There can be no greater advice! Now, let's take a look.

BABY-SITTER CLUB

One family learned from a tricky situation with a baby-sitter that the adage "To be forewarned is to be forearmed" is really true. Evidently, their 13-year-old sitter brought an R-rated video to watch while on the job. Worse, she sat 6-year-old junior next to her on the sofa while she feasted on the gorefest.

How do you prevent this? Interview your prospective sitter in advance. Share your concerns about appropriate entertainment choices with them and make it clear they are not permitted to bring any video into your house without prior permission. Then, post the "rules of the roost" on the refrigerator. Define what's permitted viewing. Make it clear how much time spent watching TV is acceptable.

In fact, copier centers such as Kinkos can laminate your list. Then using a grease pencil you can spell out the evening's plan. It can be as simple as:

1.   The shows the children are permitted are . . .
2.   The shows they may not watch are . . .
3.   The videos that are possible options tonight include . . .

I'm sure your kids are angels. But even the most angelic child will be tempted to stretch the family policy with a sitter who doesn't have direct instructions from you.

DEALING WITH DAYCARE

It's always wise to carefully select a daycare facility. But some parents make the mistake of forgetting to inquire whether or not the use of videotapes or television is incorporated into the child's routine. If they are, ask to see a copy of the titles in their video library.

Further, explore if they have a non-TV recreational option for your child. If they are unwilling to be helpful with your concern, imagine how they might deal with your child's concerns when in their care! That should be a serious red flag to find another facility.

HOTEL HAPPINESS

When you're on a family vacation, what do your kids do immediately after you check into your hotel room? Does jumping on the bed sound familiar?! Next to that sport, the swimming pool and the TV (with all of those satellite options) are both rather tempting. Have you ever found yourself facing the embarrassment of unloading the car while your kids flipped on the tube only to land on a sexually explicit cable option?

There is a way to avoid that unnecessary visual assault. We've made a practice of requesting at check-in that the front desk block all premium video and cable options from our room. Some hotels claim they aren't "in a position to provide that assistance." (I promptly inform them that "I'm not in a position to give you my money!") Which is why when I make our reservations I try to determine their ability to block in advance. If they can't, I find a hotel that *can*!

SLEEPY EYES

Overnight parties can be a barrel of fun ... at least for the kids! Games, outdoor sports, a new house to explore, and being with best friends—there's nothing like it. As a youth, I remember bundling up in a sleeping bag after a long evening of activity, only to talk and laugh halfway through the night. But that was long before the Flood ... not to mention the invention of videotape.

Today, both children and their emotionally tapped-out parents seem to get lazy and rely upon watching videotapes. If your young person is invited to spend the night at a friends, make an effort to at least meet the parents in charge. Explain that you're working hard to help your young person make wise entertainment choices—including the TV and video selections. Ask if they intend to show a movie and what's the title and rating.

If you're uncomfortable with the option, say so. Offer to provide a video you know to be a worthy choice. Obviously you don't want to insult the host. At the same time, you're under no obligation to allow your young person to participate. If the host appears uncooperative, hold a party of your own and do it the right way!

RENTAL REGULATIONS

I'm amazed at how many parents don't realize they can place a restriction on their family's video rental card. Locations such as a video counter in the supermarket or a "mom and pop" corner video store will place a block on your account that prohibits the rental of R-rated material to minors. All you have to do is ask them next time you're at the store.

A number of the national video rental chains (including Blockbuster) actually have a corporate policy of prohibiting R-rated rentals to those under 17. And a growing number of stores offer "family edited" versions of popular films.

SCHOOLING TEACHERS

Most schools send a permission slip home if a teacher plans on utilizing a popular movie with students. On the whole, our experience has been pretty good with that system. Apparently, some educators don't apply this rule of thumb if the film is rated "G"—which is supposed to make it suitable for all audiences.

One day our daughter came home and reported that her teacher showed the G-rated *Pagemaster* in class—a film we have not permitted her to view. Why? When I reviewed it for a national publication, I had concerns about the inappropriate level of violence and scary moments it contains.

Did I freak out and threaten to confront the school board? Hardly. First we talked through the experience with Carissa. We processed her feelings. Then my wife took a few extra minutes with the teacher to patiently explain our concerns. Now the teacher has assured us she'll always provide a permission slip anytime a film is shown. An even better idea would be to discuss this at the beginning of the school year.

"EX" MARKS THE TROUBLE SPOT

For readers who are divorced, it's possible that you have a unique concern. Assuming you're working hard to teach your children how to make the best possible entertainment choices, what happens when they go and spend time with your former spouse? Worse, what if that individual is not picky about the use of media in the home? Talk about a challenge!

My advice over the years has been twofold. First, try to avoid blasting your "ex." Instead, lovingly remind the children to ask Jesus to help them make good decisions while they're away from your care. Cultivate the idea that maybe they can be a good example to their dad or mom. Perhaps go as far as sending them with a few games or appropriate video selections in their backpack.

Secondly, why not befriend a couple whose marriage you admire. From time to time, have them over for dinner. Before they arrive, let them know you have the added agenda of discussing TV and video habits. As naturally as possible, allow the subject to be introduced before or after the meal. Your children can benefit by seeing that not all daddies (or mommies as the case may be) are careless with their choices. Keep in mind that many of a young person's strongest influences are heroes other than their biological parents.

THE FAMILY FEUD

I was a guest on a national radio talk show when a woman caller provided me with this dilemma. Evidently, every time her husband and children would go and spend the day at her sister's house, they'd be bombarded by televisions. In the kitchen, bathroom, bedrooms, family room, den—you name it, her sister had TVs everywhere! Making matters worse, the tubes would always be on—even if nobody was around to watch.

She also reflected that her sister becomes defensive any time the subject is raised. Have you ever had that experience? What would you do? My best advice is to have a conversation with your own children before leaving to spend the day. Encourage them to see themselves as an example of a better way. Promote the idea of them spending time outdoors playing as much as possible. And when inside, gravitate toward a room that doesn't have a set. Let your actions speak louder than your words.

Incidentally, I've spoken with families who, having anticipated these circumstances, implemented these ideas with much success. It takes a little extra effort, but it pays rich dividends.

THE SECOND WEEK
Music to Your Ears

DAY 8

Making Beautiful Music

*Striking a Responsive Chord with Your
Teenager*

*Rock 'n roll should be about rebellion. It should piss
your parents off, and it should offer some element of
taboo. It should be dangerous, you know?*

TRENT REZNOR[1]

Welcome to our second week together!
Having spent the better part of last week
on TV, do you think you're ready to tackle a
new topic? We'll be spending this week dis-
covering how to strike the right musical chord
in your home. I'm sure you've probably discovered a number of approaches that don't
work. So your goal today is learning *the right
approach* when talking about music with your
young people.

As we get started, I'd like for you to think
back to the days when you were a teenager.
Can you recall the first tape, record album, or
8-track (yikes!) you bought? Depending on
your age, remember how you were instructed
not to get your fingerprints on the record? Do
you recollect the hours you spent staring at the
photos on the album jacket or reading the

lyrics printed on the inner sleeve as you sang along when nobody was looking?

How about your favorite band or musician? When you were a teen, who was tops? Tommy Dorsey? The Everly Brothers? Elvis? The Monkees? The Stones? Carole King? The Beach Boys? The Temptations? Fleetwood Mac? The Eagles? Elton John? Bon Jovi? Bruce Springsteen? Amy Grant? Madonna? Whitney Houston? U2? And how does it make you feel *today* when *your* kids, thanks to a series of re-releases, inform you about that "new group," the Beatles?!

Did you go through a "guitar hero" stage with Jimi Hendrix, Eric Clapton, or Eddie Van Halen? What about disco? Then again, never mind. How about your parents ... did you ever find yourself in a tug-of-war over your musical taste? Are you tired of all of these questions because you want to cut to the advice on how to fix your kid's deplorable "music" rather than take this trip down memory lane?

Actually we've already begun the first step toward today's goal, which is learning *the right approach* when talking about music with our young people. After all, your first step is to realize *you've been there!* You've had a favorite album that you practically wore out ... you knew all the words and spent hours talking about the latest new group with your friends ... when possible, you might have even gone to a concert ... and you may have worked on a few dance steps too. What your children are going through is nothing new.

So why are these observations important? Because if you're like thousands of parents I've worked with over the last decade, it's likely you've forgotten what the discovery process over music was all about. The thrill is gone. In other words, the music rattling your home (with the epicenter located in your kid's room) is nothing more than a troubling nuisance. Do us both a favor. Relax. Don't panic. We'll be talking about music throughout the week, so let's take it one step at a time.

TEEN ANGEL

Don't get me wrong. When your little angel is attracted to music that sounds like it flows directly from hell, there's good reason to be concerned. But in our haste to find a quick-fix solution, two things can happen: it's easy to lose the joy that God intended for us to experience from music; and we can trash the relationship with our young people along with their music. I believe today's ideas will help you avoid making either mistake.

But if you're looking for a magic potion or easy formula this week, you'd be as naive as the story I once heard about an Amish boy and his father. One day these two guys decided to visit a mall. Being Amish and unaccustomed to the use of electricity, they were amazed by virtually everything they laid their eyes on. Of particular interest were two shiny chrome walls that had the ability to move apart and back together again.

Naturally, the wide-eyed boy asked his dad, "Father, what is this we are seeing?" Not knowing how to respond, the father answered, "Son, I cannot say I've ever seen anything like this in all my days. I don't have the first idea what it might be." Just as they were engaged in this exchange, an elderly, wheelchair-bound lady rolled up to the moving walls. They noticed after she pushed a button, the doors opened and she was able to wheel into a small room.

The walls closed and the boy and his father watched as small circles of lights with numbers lit up above the walls. They continued to watch the circles light up in the reverse direction. The walls opened up again and a beautiful 24-year-old woman stepped out.

The father said to his son, "Go get your mother!"

When it comes to the issue of today's music, wouldn't it be nice if we could just place our teens in a little room, push a few buttons, and "Voilà!"—a perfectly agreeable young person emerges! It doesn't work that way. If you're to be successful, you must be realistic as we approach the task.

BRIDGE OVER TROUBLED WATER

As a matter of fact, I'd like to keep our focus on *you* today, rather than on your children. Why? Because there are times when we parents unknowingly amplify the debate over music in the home. How? By allowing our particular motivation for addressing music to get in the way of honest evaluation. Understanding what currently motivates your decisions about musical selections will help you adjust your approach—if necessary—to a more healthy position.

I've discovered virtually all parental concern flows from one of four approaches. I call them: *Gimme Shelter, Burnin' Down the House, Que Será Será*, and *Celebrate Good Times*. See if you can identify which description fits you best:

Gimme Shelter

When it comes to popular music, these parents play the part of an ostrich. They blindly assume that if they can just shield their young people from all music and radio, somehow the problem will simply go away. Accordingly, their decisions over music in the home are motivated by **FEAR**.

Burnin' Down the House

These parents are poised for a good, long fight. As supreme rulers in the home, what they say goes—and that's that. They wrongly assume that they will be successful by demanding agreement and conformity. More often than not, their decisions regarding music are motivated by **TASTE**.

Que Será Será

These parents aren't necessarily fans of Doris Day. As a matter of fact, they're typically products of the sixties generation.

For them, that "live and let live" motto is still very much alive. Their complacency stems from the notion, "I survived the '60s; it can't be much worse today." As a result, decisions about music in the home are driven by **APATHY**.

Celebrate Good Times

For these parents, music is something very special. They fully recognize that in a fallen world there will be those musicians who abuse God's great gift. But that doesn't have to prevent them from searching for the best choices. Their thankfulness to the Lord for this treasure means decisions regarding music will be motivated by **FREEDOM**.

ROCK AROUND THE CLOCK

Okay, where do you find yourself in the spectrum of motivating factors? Be honest. If it's fear, taste, or apathy, let's see how those perspectives complicate your task.

FEAR: This can imply a lack of trust or lack of confidence in your child's ability to become discerning. Believe me, preteens and teens alike pick up the notion that you can't (or won't) count on them to exercise good judgment. Ultimately, that dogmatic position fosters curiosity. And curiosity without guidance always spells trouble.

TASTE: I'm sure you'd agree taste is subjective. In fact, our tastes can and do change. To define music in the home based primarily upon what the parents like, or what they think "sounds okay," will breed resentment. And resentment always drives a wedge between you and your teen.

APATHY: Here, the teen reasons, "My parents don't care, why should I?" After all, he or she reasons that parents are a reflection of God to the family. So this must not be an issue with God. Naturally, there's no need for teens to make any effort to be wise in their choices.

By contrast to the previous perspectives, parents who foster a sense of thankfulness and freedom create an atmosphere of *mutual dialogue* and *discovery*. In this kind of home environment, teens feel comfortable exchanging ideas about music with their parents. Why? Because it's no longer a competition. It's not a dictatorship. And it's certainly not a free-for-all.

Which is why today, if you're not there already, I'd like for you to consider adjusting your perspective toward one of freedom. It might take prayer—maybe even a little fasting—but embracing a spirit of freedom regarding music is well worth it. But what for? Simply because it works! Your home doesn't have to be a battle zone between parents and children. Does that sound like a dream too good to be true? Believe me, it *is* possible. In fact, over the next few days we'll look at specific ways to make that dream come alive in your home.

How can I be so confident?

It worked for my mom and dad—and they had 5 children!

Wise Shoppers Avoid Wise Mouths

For the Record, There's a Better Way to Shop

The manner of one's art is the banner of one's heart.

TIMOTHY WHITE[1]

Picture this. It's your son or daughter's birthday. You've been provided with a wish list of 5 CDs by musicians you never knew existed. Faced with this list, you're wondering, "Are the selections good, bad, or downright ugly? Where can a parent get reliable information to make a morally sound music purchase?"

Or imagine this scenario. Your teenager has been listening to the radio. There's a new song by Joe Rockstar and everybody is talking about it. Not surprisingly, your teen wants to pick up Joe's hot CD. You made the effort to listen to the lyrics over the airwaves and they seemed okay, but what about the album? Is there ever a difference between radio versions and the CD?

After all, in both instances you might feel unqualified to make a decision. Yet that doesn't mean you're powerless to maximize the musical purchases for your family. In fact, today we'll look at a two-step approach to make the most out of music and to help you avoid what happened to Mr. Jenkins.[2]

I met Steve Jenkins after a youth culture seminar I was conducting in Florida. At 38 years of age, he attended the presentation because of his desire to pick up a few pointers on selecting music. Evidently, he experienced a major blunder that served as a rude wake-up call. Here's what happened. Wanting to be a generous parent, he took his 12-year-old son Justin to a local record store to buy a birthday present. He told Justin to pick something out and he'd pay for it.

Elated, Justin selected a CD and promptly returned. Mr. Jenkins paid without thinking twice about the purchase and they went home. Several days later, an irate neighbor called Steve to complain that Justin was a bad influence by introducing his boy to pornographic music. Before Steve could defend himself, the neighbor said, "What's more, Justin tells me you bought him the CD!"

Flabbergasted, Steve realized he hadn't bothered to look at the choice before he purchased it. Worse, he never gave it a passing thought. After making apologies, he had to confront Justin. And learning the store had a "no return" policy, they were out of pocket the $15.

While he was retelling this situation, I kept thinking Steve could have avoided the embarrassment, received a refund, and, more importantly, the boys might not have been exposed to audio pornography if Steve had worked on becoming a wise shopper.

Would you like to avoid these kinds of problems? You can. All it takes is a little advance preparation.

SOUR NOTES

This may come as a surprise, but the best place to become a wise shopper is none other than Ma Bell's Yellow Pages. You'll need to carve out 15 quiet minutes for this process. Using a yellow legal pad along with the Yellow Pages, look under the heading "Records, Tapes, & CDs" for retailers of music. As the slogan goes, we'll let our fingers "do the walking."

Your goal is to identify a retailer who is sensitive to concerns about explicit recordings. Now, one by one, call the individual stores and ask to speak with the manager or owner. Inform him or her that you're looking for a store to bring all of your business to, but before you do, there are a few company policy matters you'd like to clarify. Here's your script:

I'm sure you're busy, but I'd appreciate it if you could help me with 4 or 5 questions . . .

> Do you sell recordings with Parental Advisory labels to minors? If so, at what age do you draw the line? Age 15? 12? 7?
>
> Can I return a recording if it has objectionable lyrical content such as profanity, the advocacy of suicide, rape, drug usage, or similarly socially adverse behavior?
>
> Do you offer the opportunity for a customer to read lyrics in advance of making a purchase?
>
> Do you have a listening station for previewing recordings?
>
> If a CD or tape that my young person brings home has pornographic images inside the sleeve, will you refund our money or offer store credit?

When you're finished, thank the managers and be sure to get their names and titles. Remember to give them the benefit of the doubt when you place the call. Keep your tone upbeat. If needed, find common ground such as, "Are you a parent? Do you have children? Are you sometimes concerned about the things they listen to? Can you see where I'm coming from?"

Once you identify a retailer who looks promising, the next step is to visit the store. Although it may have a wonderful in-house sales policy, the music outlet may also carry video tapes—even hard-core porn videotapes. I've been in numerous music stores where an entire section of triple-X videos and their explicit covers were prominently displayed in a main aisle.

Your goal is to find a music store where you can feel relatively comfortable permitting your young people to make their purchases. Likewise, we want to identify a retailer who has a decent return policy for indecent recordings. And it's a wonderful bonus when you can find a location where your questions receive helpful responses.

Going back to my original scenario (searching for a birthday present), one sign of a good store is a place that has clerks who will answer a question such as this: "My son enjoys rap music, but we have a policy in our house of not listening to obscenity. That rules out most of the current options. Can you suggest a few recent or older options that might fit the bill?"

So far, you've accomplished 3 things: (1) discovered a retailer's sales policy; (2) learned that the store's environment is relatively fitting; and (3) found a key contact for your concerns—and for musical advice. That's step 1. Part 2 involves a few thought-provoking questions for your kids.

Perhaps after dinner, maybe even during family devotions, introduce the topic of music in the house. Explain that you and your spouse desire to please the Lord with the selections the family makes. Invite your kids' participation and begin by asking the following questions. Don't forget, your role is that of advocate—not adversary.

QUESTIONS FOR KIDS

What are a few reasons you'd like to buy music?
Are there any wrong reasons to purchase music? If so, what might they be?

Did you know that when you buy a CD or tape, you're economically underwriting the artists' lifestyle and lyrical position? If they're a negative influence, does that mean you're partially responsible for the poor behavior they celebrate?

Do you think Jesus cares what kinds of things you put into your mind? Why or why not?

How might Romans 12:1–2 be applied to the music choices you make?

Remember to take the position that—just as we're working on making better television choices since last week—our family is worth the *best* when it comes to music, too. Admit that you're in need of their help. After all, our intent is to make allies out of every family member.

It's possible that your kids may still feel like there's no big deal. Or that you're an uptight parent who's making an issue out of this. If you fly into that turbulence, point them to a multi-million selling musician who shares your concern.

For example, take the popular artist named Seal, who won a Grammy for the hit single "Kiss from a Rose." He told *Entertainment Weekly*, "I don't think I would like any of my children to be exposed to some of the lyrics certain artists see fit to express in music" (3/8/96). Even if your kids are not familiar with Seal, the point is that several popular stars agree that real wisdom is to avoid the wise mouths.

Does what I've outlined sound like more work than you care to make time for? Are you beginning to wonder if all of this careful planning for purchasing music is really necessary? Just in case those thoughts are playing in your mind, let me assure you THIS IS NOT OPTIONAL! It's an often neglected yet fundamental part of parenting. And as I've witnessed over the last 15 years of my work addressing the field of popular culture, there are wonderful rewards for the families who follow that old football strategy: The Best Offense is a Good Defense.

Rewards? Like what? Like raising children who don't embrace the self-destructive ideas celebrated by morally bankrupt musicians. And having a house where young minds are not molested by rapid-fire obscenity or swayed by the rantings of an "artist" who belittles parents. And raising minds that engage their world rather than passively accept it.

Now where are those Yellow Pages?!

DAY 10

Lyrical Analysis for Amateurs

Seven Questions That Must Be Asked of Every Song

Sing and make music in your heart to the Lord.

EPH. 5:19B

Yesterday we introduced the idea of improving musical choices in your family. And assuming you fulfilled your homework assignment(!), you've located the best place to shop for CDs and tapes. Today we'll discover how to evaluate the ideas communicated in a song. We want to discover whether what we're listening to is good or bad advice, helpful or harmful, wise or foolish, pleasing to God or anathema.

As we do, you might feel like singing the blues. It's possible you're thinking, "But Bob, I can't carry a tune in a bucket. How am I supposed to carry on a conversation about music—with my kids!?" Just remember, this is lyrical analysis for *amateurs*. You don't have to have a musical bone in your body. All that's required is the desire to weigh what's being said.

The first set of questions addresses the broader picture of song writing and moral issues. The second set gets to the heart of a song. In both cases, I've provided your line of inquiry in italic type, followed by specific goals and insights to identify in regular type. As you work through them, be as formal or informal as you like. But make this a *fun* process—like looking for hidden gems. Ready? Then let's turn up the volume.

SIX PRELIMINARY QUESTIONS FOR CONSIDERATION

1. How important are lyrics in understanding what the musician desires to express? Very important? Somewhat valuable? Unnecessary?

Your purpose is to help the young listener see that lyrical ideas are actually the central focus of a song. To dismiss their study would be to overlook the whole point of music analysis and appreciation.

2. On average, do you think a musician spends a lot of time writing lyrics, or just a few minutes?

Living in Nashville alongside professional songwriters, I can attest to the fact that creative song writing sometimes comes quickly but usually requires much thought and effort. Your goal is to help your kids see that song lyrics do not happen by accident. More than likely, it's something the writer feels deeply about and worked hard to express.

3. Musicians sing about a wide range of topics. What subjects are morally offensive to you? List them and explain what makes them out-of-bounds for you.

Here, if they've never thought about it, kids may need a little prodding. Ask, "What about someone who sings about the joys of abusing children or about the fun of illegal drug usage? Are those perspectives wrong? What makes them wrong?"

4. *If a musician mocks Jesus in his music, do you think you should be listening?*

Frequently, I've worked with teens who have attempted to rationalize all other deviant topics a musician may sing about. But even the most casual Christian usually draws a line here. If not, better find out why not!

5. *If an artist devalues the very things you believe in (such as sexual purity, avoiding drunkenness, honesty), do you think over time it might have a negative effect on you?*

Don't be surprised if they say, "I know what my beliefs are and I won't be swayed." If so, bring up the story of David and Bathsheba in 2 Samuel 11. If the king of Israel can be tempted to compromise his values after one look, what makes us light-weight 20th-century Christians think we can stand firm when we're immersed in temptation?

6. *I want you to always feel free to come to me to talk about any song lyrics that troubles you. I know I might not be as "cool" as your friends, but will you promise to use me as a sounding board?*

On the surface this may appear to be unnecessary to articulate. Believe me, the fact is that teens need to know their endless questions are not a hassle to you. Open the doorway to communication as wide as possible.

Keep in mind, these 6 questions are something you probably only need to cover once in order to set the stage for responsible decision making. But the next set of questions can be used as frequently as needed.

Again, the objective is to condition your young person's mind to always *weigh what's being said* rather than to mindlessly hum along. If it makes you more comfortable, why not dust off an old record of your own—one where you *know* what is actually being sung! Then work through the questions below.

7 SIMPLE SONG CONSIDERATIONS

1. What's the subject of the song?

Take, for instance, the Aerosmith hit song a number of years ago called "Dude Looks Like a Lady." The subject of the song was a groupie who caught the attention of the singer backstage at a concert.

2. What is the song's conclusion?

When the singer decides to have casual sex with this groupie he thought was a woman, he discovers her to be really a guy. Worse, he has sex anyway.

3. Does the song recommend behavior or a perspective that's praiseworthy—or problematic? Explain.

In our Aerosmith example, without question what he celebrates is bad advice—not to mention sinful.

4. Is there a moral or social issue in this song? If so, what is said about it?

Actually, in our example there are both issues at work. On a moral level, the band is indulging in behavior that offends the Author of sex. Sin aside, it's dangerous social policy to advocate anonymous sex.

5. Do you agree or disagree with the point of the song?

Forcing your kids to vocalize their analysis is a critical step. There's something powerful that happens when they audibly state what they know in their heart.

6. If you disagree, does it make sense to fill your mind with ideas you know are wrong? And how will listening to it 50, 100, even 150 times potentially weaken your position?

We're after a similar response as in question 5 from our general questions section.

7. What specifically can you point to that demonstrates the lyrics are right or wrong?

Here's where your kids need to dig into the Scriptures—if necessary with your help. By appealing to the Bible as the final authority in your home, it's no longer a debate between you and your young people. It's a matter between them and their Creator!

One noteworthy observation. In my studies I've found a number of thoughtful insights expressed by musicians. At the same time, they felt compelled to "spice" up their image with an occasional profanity. That's been a tough call to make for many families. They don't want to say "no" to all music. Yet while the overall lyric treatment might be acceptable, the incidental profanity is unnecessary and offensive.

Columnist John Leo, who writes for *U.S. News & World Report*, confronted by this very dilemma with his own 14-year-old daughter, has real insight. He contends, "Most of the discussion of obscene music has focused on over-the-top gangsta rap and nihilistic hard rock. But it is worth focusing on the first small steps toward the breaking of norms in mainstream music—the casual insertion of a few obscenities, making them seem normal and unobjectionable."[1]

I couldn't agree more.

It's worth pointing out that edited versions of some of today's music does exist. In the fall of 1996, Wal-Mart made headlines because their corporate policy required these offensive elements to be removed—or they wouldn't sell the recordings! You might consider shopping at Wal-Mart or another retailer who requires the artists to clean up their act.

As you and your young people work at making better musical choices, two Scriptures are worth using as guiding principles: Matthew 12:36–37 in which the Lord reminds us we'll be responsible for "every careless word" that we speak (I imagine that would including singing!), and Colossians 3:1–2, 5–6, which encourages us to "Set your minds on things above, not on earthly things."

Feedback and Faithful Fathering

What to Do When Your Parental Approach Skips a Beat

I'm acutely aware of fear and betrayal. My father had a bad relationship with his mother. She had left his father at an early age, so he was keenly attuned to her betrayal of him. I think that's something that was passed down.

CHRIS CARTER, "X-FILES" CREATOR[1]

How did your conversation regarding lyrics go with the kids yesterday? As smooth as silk? Or downright discouraging? Please understand that a certain degree of frustration and resistance is to be expected. Especially if their craniums haven't been creatively stretched in a while. But, assuming they have a relationship with the Lord, outright hostility or anger might be indicative of a deeper dynamic: parental resentment. Which reminds me of Paula.

Paula was a 16-year-old girl I spoke with after a seminar on pop culture. I remember her distinctly because of the outright hatred she felt toward her parents. Evidently, they ignored her due to their crazy work schedules. They couldn't make time to see her school play. Her birthday was greeted with a last minute store-bought cake and belated card. Because they were too busy to eat together even once a week, their house resembled a motel more than a home.

One day Paula's parents read an article on the decline in American entertainment and decided to get "all hot and bothered about it"—in Paula's words. All of a sudden they wanted to have "deep, meaningful talks" about "what I was doing with my music," she recalled. Listening to a lecture on musical lewdness by her "frantic" parents, Paula said, "I couldn't help but wonder, Where had they been the last five years of my life? Why should I listen to them now as they describe something important to *them* after they spent years ignoring all that was important to *me?*"

Ouch!

I don't excuse Paula for her poor choices. At the same time I certainly empathize with those very real feelings of resentment—feelings that get in the way of any attempt at demonstrating love and concern in this arena. That's why today I'd like for us to evaluate and strengthen the vitality of our parent-child relationships.

SONS OF THUNDER

If I met your son or daughter after a seminar, how might they describe their relationship with you? Why is that important? I'm convinced there is no greater influence upon a young person's self-esteem and personal decision-making process (especially those relating to music) than parental acceptance and affirmation. According to various reports I've reviewed, in families where teenagers feel unconditional love and are self-confident, experimentation with destructive and addictive behaviors is minimized—which makes complete sense.

I remember speaking to a class of teens at a Christian school concerning this topic. I spent a few minutes asking them about their musical choices. Then I asked them to rate their relationships with their fathers. As I studied their comments, I found two primary responses: Either they loved their fathers or they *hated* them. Furthermore, those who had solid relationships with their dads tended to accept, and even invite, parental participation on the issue of music. Those with a poor relationship always resented any such involvement.

Take a moment to eavesdrop on several of their perspectives. We'll start with a few bad parental reviews. Even though they're negative, they can be instructional if only we have the ears to hear.

Gary said, "My father is emotionally and verbally abusive to me. There's no way I could ever talk about personal stuff with him. I never had a good male father figure." One girl who had seriously contemplated suicide explained, "I find myself wishing that my parents would either get divorced so I don't have to be scared of my dad, or kick me out of the house. But I've never given them a reason to ask me to leave. All of my problems and rebellions I keep hidden from them because I'm ashamed."

Stephanie shared, "I guess my dad doesn't know how to show love or express his feelings. Maybe someday he and I will be like a true father and daughter should be. Until then, the distance between us keeps our conversations pretty shallow." Darla didn't hesitate as she observed, "I just wish my dad made time for me. When he talks he's always impatient so I don't bother to convey my honest feelings. If I did try, he'd just cut me off."

Aaron explained, "My relationship with my father is not very good. We don't know each other. And I don't want to let him get to know me. We have no significant communication, so I can't really go to him for godly council or advice. I believe the most important issue is for the father to be the spiritual leader. I guess I'm just bitter!"

Pause for a moment to reflect: Do you think these young people would find themselves open to parental guidance on something as personal as "their music" when they can't—or don't care to—talk with their dads? Taking it a step further, might it be possible that a teen's poor musical choice exists as a form of passive-aggressive behavior? In other words, in their pain and disappointment over the lack of parental love or approval, might they "protest" by withdrawing into "rebellious" music? Is it really surprising when a child raised in this environment resists loving instruction?

YOU LIGHT UP MY LIFE

By contrast, when students gave their fathers high marks for spiritual leadership, I found it *did* make a big difference in their openness to talk about entertainment. Christy said, "My dad and I are great friends. We enjoy teasing each other and giving one another a hard time. In the summer, we go fly-fishing a lot and talk about my life, school, going to concerts—important stuff like that. Every morning my dad leads prayer with the family before we go to school."

Larry confided, "I love my dad. He cares for me. While guys at school appear to like to bash their dad, I have a good relationship with mine. We go golfing every Saturday where we talk about things. My dad is forever a friend—even when he's forcing me to think about my music." Renee views her dad as "the sweetest, most generous, supportive, and understanding person in the whole world. I'm very close to him and I love him dearly. I trust him with all of my heart and I respect his wisdom on things like the stuff I put into my head."

Jerry considered his dad to be his "best friend. We argue sometimes, but that's normal. He hasn't forgotten what it's like to be a teenager. He understands when I talk to him about my music and my personal stuff. He's great."

Carry's comment grabbed me by the throat. She explained, "Every night he tells me, 'I love you.' After dinner, on the nights we eat together as a family, he leads us in a little Bible study. Sometimes he uses a popular song or TV show when applying the Scriptures to my world. He sincerely loves Jesus and encourages me to do the same throughout my life."

In spite of the powerful media influences that fill his world, Doug maintains, "My father has instilled in me the values that I hold today—especially when I'm plugged into my headphones." Lastly, there's John, who paid his father the ultimate tribute: "My father is my role model. He's the godliest man I know. My greatest fear is thinking of life without him whenever God decides it's time for him to graduate to glory."

Frankly, these kids speak for me. They describe the relationship I had with my parents as I grew up, and maintain to this day.

Upon closer inspection, according to these teens the keys to unlocking mutual respect could be summarized as follows:

Playful banter; less lecture.
Time alone enjoying a relaxed, shared experience
Daily doses of "I love you"
Appropriate challenges to follow Jesus
Consistent prayer
Regular devotions with current events naturally worked into
    the discussion from time to time

What do you do if, after evaluating your parent-child relationship in light of this chapter, you decide there's room for serious improvement? Consider taking small steps to rebuild the bridges of healthy communication. Strengthen the vitality of your relationship by introducing one or more of the above 6 dynamics. You could begin *today* by uttering those 3 magical words that no teen can hear enough—I love you.

In the absence of hearing that from you, anything else you might attempt to communicate about culture is likely to be received as nothing more than unwelcome feedback. After all, our children are not projects that need "fixing," they're gifts from God—gifts that require faithful fathering.

A Little Sound Advice

Setting the Right Stage for Concert-Goers

We become what we are continually exposed to. Every experience of life is recorded by the mind's camera lens on archival tape, there to wait patiently until called for.

JOE WHEELER[1]

Can you remember the first time you went to a rock concert? Do you recall what it was like? The earliest memories I have of catching a band in concert was at our hometown YMCA in Philadelphia. I was 13. That afternoon my best friend and I rode our bikes to the "Y" to shoot some hoops. I recall hearing the music as we approached. A band was jamming on Iron Butterfly's 21-minute "In-A-Gadda-Da-Vida."

Although I forget the name of that local group, I recollect those guys had no fancy lights, no fog machines, no pulsating lasers . . . and, come to think about it, they didn't grab their crotches.

Teens attending a concert today are in for a very different experience. One concert event I attended demonstrates how times have changed. With the crowd of more than 17,000 hooting and hollering approval, the guitarist on stage dropped his pants and "mooned" the audience. I turned to a nearby police officer and asked, "If I dropped my drawers right here in public, would you arrest me?" He answered, "Yes, without hesitation." Why? Because, he informed me, it's a violation of public decency laws.

I then asked, "If that's the case, why don't you arrest the musician on stage who has his pants currently around his ankles?" With a straight face he explained that "When *they* do it, it's art." Hmm.

I was struck by several things (including the heavy smell of marijuana wafting over from the couple next to me). First, parents send their kids to concerts with little or no guidance. Second, parents don't adequately prepare their kids for potentially dangerous crowd dynamics. Third, nudity and sexual situations onstage are far more commonplace than most parents would realize.

For example, Twiggy, a bandmate of the controversial metal act Marilyn Manson, described one of their shows in these terms: "The cops also made a big deal about a show where Marilyn put some guys d—k in his mouth on-stage. But we've done much worse things than that. I had my 11-year-old brother on-stage in one of the shows completely naked. It was like child pornography."[2] (By the way, Marilyn Manson is a guy whose real name is Brian Warner. Brian derived his stage name by combining the personas of Marilyn Monroe and Charles Manson.)

That's why today I'd like to challenge you to educate yourself on this topic. Just for "fun" make plans to attend a concert that you'd never personally pick. Not someone safe like white-collar rocker Bruce Springsteen. Try an alternative, metal, or rap act. Go either by yourself or with a peer. Leave your teen at home this time. You're on a reconnaissance mission. Oh, and don't forget the earplugs!

If you have an opportunity, walk around the auditorium and make a few mental notes. If it's a "dance concert" (that is, the absence of chairs) make your way into the middle of the crowd. Experience that throbbing, sweaty environment. Does it feel safe or threatening? Can you picture your youngster there? Explore the bathroom situation. Are illegal drugs or alcohol used therein? Keep an eye on the level or lack of security.

You see, over the years I've attended a wide range of concerts in several states. Some were for personal pleasure, while most were for purposes of youth culture research.[3] Along the way, I've made numerous observations about today's concert dynamic. I realize you may not feel comfortable with my suggestion to preview a concert. So, to maximize your family's concert-going, I've identified 10 tips from all of my trips:

Ear Invasion

You've probably experienced a ringing sensation in your ears after a concert. Medically speaking, this is called threshold shift and it can be the beginning sign of ear damage. Exposure to noise levels above 85 decibels (db) is harmful.

How loud is loud? A large orchestra averages 90 db at 25 yards away. Many live rock concerts, a thunderclap, and some power tools average 110 db. An airport runway clocks in at 120 db. A person must be exposed to noise at 85 db for eight hours before permanent ear damage begins. But at 105 db, ears can be damaged in just 30 minutes. Bottom line, always bring ear plugs to concert events.

Three's Company

I've spoken with private security officers who work at major rock concerts. They underline the importance of never sending a girl to a concert alone. Although chances are good there won't be any threatening circumstances, they suggest girls attend in groups of 3, and boys in twos.

Musical Chairs

There are 4 ways tickets are sold for a concert: assigned seating, sectional seating, festival-style seating, and the dance concert. The best option is when the ticket holder is assigned a specific seat. The second best approach is sectional seating. Essentially, your ticket admits you to any seat in a specific section of the venue. The third choice is festival-style, which is basically general admission. The problems include losing track of others in your group (since there are no seat numbers), and the race to get the best location can resemble a shoving match. The worst method of selling seats is the dance concert. What makes this downright dangerous is the lack of seats! A sea of humanity is thrown into an area where—if you push hard enough—you can make your way to the front of the stage. Avoid at all cost.

Bathroom Bust

A sad reality at far too many events is the use of bathrooms to traffic in drugs. There have been situations where an innocent concert-goer was arrested in a bathroom during a police round-up due to guilt by association. If you see something that appears to be an illegal drug transaction, leave. And report the unusual activity to the authorities.

Putting Parents in their Place

In the late '80s, a movement by concerned parents sparked the creation of "parent rooms" at concert halls. These glorified smoking lounges were equipped with a TV and folding chairs so that parents could wait for their young people until after the concert. My view is that a parent tucked away from the action in this fashion serves as little more than a taxi service. I'd recommend the parent make the effort to attend the show and share the concert experience.

Don't Park on a Lark

Many concert halls are located in dilapidated, poorly lit sections of town. Finding a parking spot may require walking some distance through an unsafe area late at night after the show. With a little advance planning of locating a nearby parking structure, you and your loved ones won't be put at added risk. Thankfully, newer facilities are required in most cities to provide an abundance of parking adjacent to the venue.

Ticket Trouble

Buying tickets from scalpers is illegal in virtually every state. Aside from the possibility of your purchasing bogus tickets (which is a common occurrence), some scalpers are more interested in your open wallet. As the unsuspecting customers reach in their purses or wallets, these characters grab their goods and run for cover down a preplanned escape route. It's always best to make your purchase from official dealers before the show.

Locate Exits

I've made it my policy to note where at least two exits are in case of an emergency in the dark. Remember, once the concert begins, the lights go out. Finding a fast exit location can be very difficult under those circumstances.

Moshing and Other Pit Falls

Two common activities amongst today's young fans are moshing and stage diving. Moshing is sort of playing an unorganized game of rugby to loud music. Fans flail about, thrashing into each other with reckless abandon. Broken fingers and sprained ankles are a common by-product. Worse, gashed eyes, concussions, and even sexual groping have been reported.

Stage diving, though a different activity, yields many of the same results—and even death. An individual climbs up onto the stage or nearby scaffolding and throws himself onto the mercy of the crazed audience. If they don't catch the diver, he will end up on the floor with a bruised or broken body. Both activities are unadvised. Not to over spiritualize the issue, but 1 Thessalonians 4:4 offers a worthy reminder: "Each of you should learn to control his own body in a way that is holy and honorable."

Bulk Up on the Bible

This might be something for the more spiritually mature teen. I remember how my friends and I would go prepared to witness to the band after the event! On several occasions we followed the group back to their hotel and actually shared Christ with them at the bar. (Guess I've always hung out with radical friends!)

Although you might not have the immediate need for these 10 tips, I'm sure they'll come in handy down the road. But, as I've outlined, those who are unprepared literally risk physical abuse, robbery, and even death in some circumstances. It's up to you to instruct your clan how to make the most out of a concert. If you're properly equipped, going to a show can be an educational and possibly even enjoyable experience.

It's Showtime!

Encouraging Teens to Sound Off

The process of writing, any form of creativity, is a power intensifying life.

RITA MAE BROWN[1]

We've spent the better part of this week evaluating the music created by popular artists. Believe it or not, discussing contemporary music with young people is the *easy* part. Critiquing is always the easier path to walk than creating. That's why today I'd like to take a different approach. If you're up for it, let's explore *creating* original music as another instrument in your tool box.

Why in the world would you ever make that a priority? Simple. When young people learn how to express themselves through song, they're no longer held captive by canned, store-bought musical musings. They have an outlet for their feelings, one in which they can take pride. Further, when an individual attempts to write a song, he or she instinctively sees the value of listening more carefully to how others penned their compositions. The study of words takes on new meaning.

Where to start? Start where you are.

I'm referring to the fact that you and your family may be new to this songwriting thing. It might feel a bit far-fetched, even completely crazy. That's okay as long as you make the effort to try. Why not begin by rewriting the words to a popular song? Choose a familiar tune, preferably one that contains a few words or ideas with which you disagree. Then change the words into something more fitting. Most of all, enjoy the process!

A RECORD IDEA

As a teenager, for example, I rewrote the words to "Cocaine," a popular song written by J. J. Cale and performed by Eric Clapton. I loved the music, but disagreed with the pro-drug message. In fact, I decided to put Christian lyrics to "Cocaine" and renamed the tune, "Get Saved!" A number of years later, I recorded my version (after obtaining permission from J. J. Cale) and pressed a few thousand vinyl 45s. For fun, I released it to Christian radio stations.

It was an incredible experience watching "Get Saved!" climb the Christian music charts—ultimately becoming a number seven national hit! Don't get too excited—I didn't make any money and nobody is asking for an autograph. The real thrill for me was moving from a passive consumer to an active participant.

Keep in mind you can conduct this little writing experience at the table after dinner. Invite each young person to bring a song that they'd like to rewrite. Provide pens and yellow legal pads and let them cut loose. If you're really interested in maximizing the writing session, I'd encourage you to purchase a rhyming dictionary for about ten bucks.

For the family that has a touch of musical talent, consider collaborating on an original composition. If appropriate, divide the lyrical and musical writing responsibilities between the individual who is good with words or gifted on an instrument. Truthfully, there's an art to great songwriting. I'm not suggesting that your goal is to create a hit song—although that would be a bonus! Your objective is to encourage the experience of *creating*.

If all of this sounds a bit far-fetched to your young people, share with them the story of the Christian recording group Jars of Clay. Virtually a household name in Christian homes today, Jars had their roots in a college music class. When given the assignment to write a few songs, these guys really applied themselves. Impressed with what they submitted, professors and fellow students alike encouraged these college boys to perform live.

As God would have it, Jars played in public less than a dozen times before becoming signed to a record deal. That humble beginning blossomed into more than a million CDs and tapes sold—in addition to widespread Christian and mass market radio air play.

PIANO MAN

In the DeMoss household, my parents offered to underwrite musical lessons for my siblings and me. That encouragement—including the purchase of a family piano—is something I cherish to this day. Without their prodding, I imagine the five of us kids would have lived life musically illiterate.

Instead, sister Becky took up piano, and later guitar. Brother Steve was always good on the bongos and developed a knack for guitar. Brother Timmy went on to be the best pianist in the family—and he wasn't too shabby on drums. It took a while, but brother John has gravitated to the piano. I enjoyed formal clarinet and guitar lessons, and still mess around on drums.

Nowadays, with the popularity of low-cost home studios, along with your encouragement, who knows? The aspiring artist in your family may just be the next Jars of Clay, Michael W. Smith, or even another Amy Grant. And, come to think of it, I'll only need 10% of the royalties for giving you the idea!

DAY 14

Soul-Searching Songs

A Unique Way to Reach for the "Stars"

How, then, can they call on the one they have not believed in? And how can they believe in the one of whom they have not heard? And how can they hear without someone preaching to them?

ROM. 10:14

Have you ever wished that your kids would capture a vision for unbelievers? Do you hear them insert generic, catch-all prayer thoughts such as "Lord, bless all the mission fields," and yet you long for them to have a deeper passion for the unsaved? Is it frustrating that nothing seems to spark a hunger for the hurting souls around them at school?

I empathize with you. My wife and I pray for our daughter (and any other children the Lord may add to our quiver down the road) to embrace that kind of kingdom participation and excitement. That's why today, in our final conversation on music, I'd like to offer an idea that may spark a fire for lost souls.

Actually, this is an idea that I first had a number of years ago when I met a teen named Pam. Pam attended a small parochial school where I was speaking to the student body about music and media. One look at Pam's jean jacket, you'd think she was the personal manager of Prince—also known as "that symbol guy." From collar to cuff, her coat was covered with every Prince button ever produced.

At one point in the presentation, I unrolled a giant Prince poster—bad idea! Pam jumped up out of her seat and would have planted a kiss on his photo if I hadn't held her at bay. Yes, Pam loves Prince. Maybe *worships* is a more appropriate adjective. As a matter of fact, I've learned to love Prince as well, but for completely different reasons.

In Matthew 5:43–44, Jesus said, "There is a saying, 'Love your friends and hate your enemies.' But I say; Love your enemies! Pray for those who persecute you" (TLB)! Here's the implication for today's discussion. As much as you and I may be upset, saddened, or angered by the work of musicians who don't know the Lord, we're still commanded to love and pray for them.

Given this scriptural mandate, I now love Prince—yet I hate what he's doing through his music. (He's the singer who sings about the joys of incest.) Likewise, it's this command that prompts me to pray regularly for him as well as many other popular artists.

In fact, I've taken it a step further. For more than 10 years I've encouraged teenagers to join me in praying for today's popular musicians—in essence, to become a "Rock Star Missionary." I must confess I've been so pleased with their responsiveness. It appears whenever I make that suggestion, it's largely received with incredible enthusiasm.

SHOW ME THE WAY

Here's how it could work in your home. For starters, dust off an old Kansas tape with the song "Dust In The Wind." Listen to the words with your family. Point out how the lyrics speak of the futility of life and almost cry for spiritual direction. Explain that it was written by Kansas guitarist Kerry Livgren, who was searching for the meaning of life. And report that he has since become a believer in Christ.

Or you could read them these lyrics from the song "Show Me the Way" by super group Styx: "Every night I say a prayer in the hopes that there's a heaven ... and I feel this emptiness inside ... show me the way, take me tonight and wash my illusions away." Joan Osborne's "What If God Was One of Us" comes to mind as another prime example. Then there's U2 who yearns for heavenly intervention in "Wake Up Dead Man": "Jesus, Jesus, help me. I'm alone in this world, and a f——ed-up world it is. Tell me the story, the one about eternity and the way it's all gonna be."

The key is to find an appropriate illustration of a superstar's search for the meaning of life. Then engage your young people in a discussion along these lines: On the surface, doesn't it appear that the stars have it all together? They've got it made. Fancy limos and cars. First class accommodations. Designer clothes. Millions of CDs sold. Adoring fans around the world. They get to go to all the right parties. Life is good. Or is it?

If life is so picture perfect, why are they longing for more? Could it be the nudging of God's Spirit in their hearts, which reminds them, "What good is it for a man to gain the whole world, yet forfeit his soul?" (Mark 8:36). Do you realize that what they're missing is the very thing we have—peace and forgiveness through a relationship with Jesus! Wow. We have something these guys lack. They may be onstage, but we have the applause of heaven cheering us onward.

Now challenge your children to get a few friends (or maybe even their entire youth group) to make a locker-sized prayer calendar. Have them write the names of 30 unsaved musicians, one for each day of the month. Then pray that the Lord brings someone into the life of that day's target artist to introduce him or her to the person of Jesus. Ask that the Author of music put a new song in these musicians' hearts.

If your kids hesitate, tell them to be selfish. If they really enjoy the music of a particular band, your young person ought to pray for the band's salvation—so that the group will be around for all of eternity making music in heaven for them too.

FAITH AND FAN MAIL

For the young person who really catches the vision, suggest that they e-mail or write a letter to the band explaining what Jesus has done for them. Both kinds of addresses are usually found in teen magazines (such as *Creem*, *Hit Parader*, *Star Hits*, and *Tiger Beat*) or on the album jacket. Since some of the addresses are used for merchandising groupie paraphernalia, help your teens look for the best address.

When your kids write, encourage them to start by mentioning that the artist's song "so-and-so" prompted the desire to share what they've discovered as a follower of Jesus. I'd avoid being condemning. Instead, concentrate on ministering the love of Jesus to them. If your kids are concerned that "the musician will never see my letter," it's guaranteed the artist won't if the letter is never written! However, by taking the time to write, your son or daughter opens the door for the Holy Spirit to work. Wouldn't it be awesome if a popular performer made a commitment to Christ as a result of your child's faithful witness?

By the way, I'll never forget the day my office received a phone call from Carol Bon Jovi—the mother of son Jon, the lead vocalist for super group Bon Jovi. As the person responsible for Bon Jovi's fan mail, Carol was wondering why her son was receiving so many letters about giving his heart to Christ. It just so happened that I was challenging teens to write the band through a column I penned and the readers rose to the challenge!

If you follow today's idea, I sincerely believe you'll be in a fantastic position to nurture a kingdom vision in the hearts of your children.

THE THIRD WEEK
Taking On Other Contenders

DAY 15

Cinema or "Sin-ema"

A New Technique to Really Get the Picture

I'm always amazed that people will actually choose to sit in front of the television and just be savaged by stuff that belittles their intelligence.

ALICE WALKER[1]

When was the last time you walked out of a movie? Of course, I'm not asking about your leaving at the end of the picture. I'm referring to exiting right in the middle of the action. Why did you leave? Was it a predictably boring film? Or was there something that so offended you it drove you to action?

Looking back over the last couple of years, I can identify 3 times when I headed to the back door shortly after the picture began. Interestingly, each of the films I turned my back on received the thumbs-up from highly acclaimed, nationally-trusted and respected film critics: *Natural Born Killers*, *Pulp Fiction*, and *The Crow*.[2]

Keep in mind, my occupation is that of a film and media commentator. As such, it's my job to review upwards of 100 new movie releases a year. Frankly, the overwhelming

99

majority are riddled with offensive, anti-social, or deviant elements. But since it's my vocation, I wade through the show as best I can—sometimes closing my eyes and plugging my ears for extended periods of time. So it must be seriously offensive for me to leave a theater!

The sad truth is many of us *publicly* express outrage over the trashy material Hollywood inflicts upon us, but *privately* we entertain ourselves with films that mock our values and trash the truth. I believe more of us need work on keeping our public morality in sync with our private conduct. Why? As a sign of personal integrity that helps our children to see "we're a family that walks the talk." To that end, today we're going to *learn how to watch a movie.*

Even as you read our goal it's possible the thought might come to mind, "Uh, Bob, we already know how to do that—*that's* precisely our problem. We watch a myriad of movies already!" Perhaps. But I'm fairly certain you've never viewed one the way I do. And, once you start this process, I believe you and your family will maximize the viewing experience.

Aside from the matter of personal integrity, why is this important? Author Joe Wheeler said it best. He warns, "We become what we are continually exposed to. Every experience of life is recorded by the mind's camera lens on archival tape, there to wait patiently until called for."[3] Learning how to properly process what we see in a movie helps to defuse the time bomb of dangerous mental conditioning.

SCREEN PLAY

In your mind, what are the primary "tools" associated with movie watching? If you answered popcorn, Red Hots, and a soda you'd be missing a few key items. To view a movie the way that I watch, you'll also need a clipboard, a sheet of notebook paper, and something with which to write. I've found that a penlight is also an invaluable tool—and costs less than a couple of bucks.

We begin by creating a movie guide. Divide your paper into 4 sections by drawing a horizontal line across the middle of the page and a vertical line intersecting it in the center. Your page should look like this:

Movie Vitals	Language
Positive	Negative

In the upper left box write "Movie Vitals." Across the upper right square write "Language." Write "Positive" in the bottom left and "Negative" in the remaining space. Now you're almost ready to watch a movie. Since this page will be used to keep track of key elements of the film, you may want to write several abbreviations for profanity in the "Language" section. If you've never done this, you'll be amazed at the gratuitous use of profanities in motion pictures these days.

I use this self-explanatory simple code: Fu—, Sh—, damn, GD, a—, bitch, hell, God, Christ, and Jesus. (Obviously, we only keep track of the references to deity when spoken as an expletive.) Just write the key words down one side of the box. Then, any time you hear the use of profanity, place a mark by the appropriate word, keeping a running tally throughout the film.

As you wait for the movie to begin, take a minute to fill in a few of the "Movie Vitals." For example, write the name of the film, its rating, and the names of the key characters. You can usually find that information on the poster in the theater lobby, a newspaper review, or similar promotional piece provided by the cinema. After the film, use the remaining space to write a summary of what it was about.

Once the movie begins, be listening for anything that strikes you as a positive or negative message. Jot down short notes in the appropriate box. You could make the notation: *Affirms honesty, clergy portrayed in positive light*, and, *Demonstrates that the ends don't justify the means* in the "Positive" category. Likewise place *Drug usage, Unnecessarily gruesome violence*, and, *Adulterous encounter* in the "Negative" section.

It may sound like a lot of work. But I've discovered that it forces me to pay greater attention. Why? When I take notes, my mind is actively engaged in the viewing process. I'm no longer a passive consumer. To demonstrate how easy it is, take a look at an example of my notes for the hit movie *Liar, Liar* starring Jim Carrey.

As you can see, I added a biblical application point. And to maximize the value of your research, instead of a yellow legal pad, consider using paper that has holes to fit a 3-ring binder. You'll be able to save your observations in a handy notebook for later usage. For instance, your remarks could assist a friend who would like your opinion of the film. Additionally, you'll be able to consult your notes when the video is released in several months and your young people want to rent it but you can't recall whether or not it is a worthy film.

"Liar, Liar"

MOVIE VITALS	LANGUAGE
Jim Carrey, Cary Elwes, Jennifer Tilly. PG–13. Fletcher Reede (Carrey) is a fast-talking lawyer who is never truthful. A birthday wish for one day of honesty forces him to tell the truth.	GD: 1x Sh—: 3x D—khead: 3x Fu—: 0
POSITIVE	**NEGATIVE**
Challenges the idea that lying is necessary in life. Deals with work vs. family priorities. Numerous crazy sight-gags. Loads of fun. **Application:** 1 Peter 3:10 "For, 'Whoever would love life and see good days must keep his tongue from evil & his lips from deceitful speech.'"	Sexual humor. One act of fornication (non-explicit situation). Humor turns crass at times. Divorce dynamics played for laughs.

MOVIE TRIVIA

Several friends joined me as I went to review a hit movie. They showed up with armfuls of munchies, and I had popcorn and my notebook. Afterward, I asked them to explain what was good about the film. Admittedly, they did a decent job replaying the facts. I found it interesting when they commented, "You know, there wasn't all that much bad about it." Really? Consulting my notes, there were dozens of troubling aspects. For instance, I had counted 34 "f" words—which averaged one every 3 minutes.

I then asked my friends if they recalled hearing that word spoken at any point during the day. "No" was their response. Did they use the word themselves at any point that day? Again, no. The implication was clear: They wouldn't have heard such foul language *unless they went to a movie.*

Further, to enjoy the benefits of the picture, they had to wade through a significant level of decadent speech. What other way might they have realized that same level of joy without the debauchery? The key is to use your movie guide to prompt questions for discussion later.

After you've had a chance to "work out the bugs" with this approach to viewing, consider taking your kids to an age-appropriate film and teach them to use the movie guide. Afterward, grab a pizza and review your notes together. Play the role of coach and draw out their insights. You'll find it's a fun and rewarding way to instill and nurture their spirit of discernment.

Magazine Madness

Reading Between the Lies in the Lines

I keep reading between the lies.

GOODMAN ACE[1]

How many magazines land in your mailbox each month? I think my family subscribes to 10 or 20 (not to mention the junk mail publications we didn't request). I probably order a new magazine just about every time Ed McMahon sends me a brightly colored notice informing me: "The DeMoss Family Has Won $10 Million" (and in much smaller print "if you have the winning numbers"). As they say, you just never know . . .

While plowing through my stack of magazines, I was surprised at the number of articles in which the writer and I had a fundamental difference of opinion. Upon reflection, an interesting thought struck me. See if you'd agree. It's easy to identify the use of profanity, gratuitous violence, sexual situations, and irreverence in television shows or in today's movies. These elements are an obvious affront to my family's value system.

But by contrast I must confess it can be difficult to perceive the more *subtle* attacks on my faith and family when they come sandwiched between the pages of my favorite periodicals. In other words, rarely do I find profanity in print. Yet the tendentious ideas that are sometimes promoted as truth can be equally profane. Have you noticed that, too?

Furthermore, if I as an adult have occasional trouble sorting out a story's bias from the truth, how can I expect my children to be discerning as they flip through the pages? How, indeed, unless I instruct them to comprehend what they're reading? And if they fail to receive guidance in this area, it's likely their belief system is open to yet another source of attack. Today, we'll discover how to teach our young people to read between the lines.

UNFASHIONABLE PERSPECTIVES

For this exercise to succeed, find a magazine of general interest that aligns itself with the particular interests of your son or daughter. Forgive my shameless stereotyping, but for a 15-year-old girl your technical journal will hold less interest than *Seventeen*, *Sassy*, *YM*, *Teen* or *Vogue*. Likewise, a sporting, music, or muscle magazine is likely to attract the attention of an adolescent male. If they don't already receive any magazines, scan the magazine rack for an appropriate choice.

For the purposes of illustration, I've selected an issue of *Teen*.[2] In between fashion advice, tips on how to flirt with boys, and general gossip, this issue pushed abortion onto its 1.8 million subscribers. Let's take a minute to review the article. I'll concede that the writer begins by saying the decision to abort the unborn is the "kind every girl hopes to avoid and some girls could never make." So far, so good. However, a careful reading reveals a highly biased report.

When you find an article such as this, begin by reading it with your teens. Then, assume the role of coach and draw out the thoughts of your kids. Wait until after they've had the opportunity to express themselves. Don't push them. If they smell that you have an agenda, they may be inclined to rush their ideas for fear you're not really interested. At the right moment, draw them out with a perspective they might not have considered.

Let's role play this for a minute. I'll provide several excerpts from the article and then demonstrate the kinds of insights you might be able to offer—*if* your teen doesn't think of the ideas first!

"I was lucky. The doctor informed me that I was still within the 'safe' period for having a low-risk abortion."

You might ask, "safe" and "low-risk" for whom? The mother? The unborn child? Isn't it true that for an abortion to work, a death is always involved? Why didn't the writer mention that fact?

"She asked me a lot of questions . . . to ensure that no one was coercing me into terminating my pregnancy."

Here you could raise a question about the writer's choice of words. Specifically, notice the word "terminate." What other word could have been used? Isn't it true that you terminate a flight, but you kill a baby? Why is she manipulating the words like this?

"Then we went over charts that explained how this procedure was far less traumatic than childbirth and about as life-threatening as having a penicillin shot."

Is the writer implying that the baby doesn't experience any trauma as his or her life is forcibly taken away? And, once again, the writer is missing the obvious point that abortion is *always* life-threatening to the child. Why does she keep hiding that fact from us?

"I'm grateful I live in a time and place where it was possible, albeit costly, to make my own choice."

What is the cost to which this woman is referring? The $375 for her abortion? Or the cost of a life? Which do you think is more valuable? Could you argue that life is priceless?

WORD PLAY

Isn't it amazing how a seemingly innocent magazine for teenage girls contains such a pro-abortion message? As you bring closure to your conversation, it's worth pointing out that the editors did not include an article from a teen girl who made the decision to tough it out and carry her baby to term. Nor were there sidebars on fetal development, adoption options, or a look at the potential lifelong psychological consequences of abortion.

After discussing these ideas, your next task would be to find a scripture that might speak to support your perspective. In the above instance, Psalm 139:13 comes to mind. Here, the psalmist underlines the fact that the fingerprint of God is on every life: "For you created my inmost being; you knit me together in my mother's womb."

Whether the article you select for study deals with abortion, sexuality, peer pressure, substance abuse, or matters of faith, your approach will be the same: Identify the bias of the writer, ask leading questions about their choice of words, and stimulate discussion based on the standard of scripture.

Personally speaking, I cherished the times when my father or mother would walk me through this type of evaluation. Several things happened as they did. First, it demonstrated the wisdom of my parents. Second, it taught me to read with guarded eyes—to always look for the hidden agenda. And third, it prevented the subtle manipulation of my values.

If you apply today's exercise with your kids, I'm confident you'll reap similar benefits. (Oh, and if Ed McMahon comes knocking at your door with that 10-foot grand prize check, don't forget us little guys.)

Virtuous Video Veggies

What to Do When Computer Games Aren't Child's Play

On a cost-per-kill basis, [computer game] Quake is the most cathartic experience you can legally have within the confines of your own home.

BOB STRAUSS, REVIEWER[1]

Do you remember when Space Invaders invaded game rooms? How about Asteroids and Pac Man? Those primitive coin-operated video games set the stage for a decade-long, multi-billion dollar battle for your kids' quarters. Although the joysticks are still jumping at mom and pop arcades, the real contest is for control of the home computer game market.

While Nintendo, Sega-Genesis and Atari go head-to-head with killer graphics and 3-dimensional visuals, personal computers have proven themselves a worthy competitor for the gaming dollar. An entire industry of computer video games has sailed into hyperspace, many with the added feature of play in cyberspace with on-line opponents.

As you'll discover in today's chapter, the issue of video games for children is larger than zapping aliens or blasting bad guys. Our closer inspection of today's video game diet may make you sick. But we'll also find how you can make the most of the action.

ZAP FLAP

In the late 80s, the level of violence, profanity, and even nudity in kids' video games prompted a public outcry. The martial arts-oriented selections such as "Mortal Kombat" (which featured cartoonish decapitations, impalings, and the mantra "Finish him!") sparked much of the controversy. But the likes of "Night Breed" took terror to a new level. It had a subplot of hanging college coeds on meat hooks. Likewise, "Phantasmagoria" includes a rape sequence.

This genre of games prompted several national news organizations to take to the airwaves to help parents fight back. The results? To the best of my research, you and I have been handed an ambiguous, self-regulated, and inconsistent rating system for video games. As of this writing, there are 2 regulatory agencies: the Rating System Advisory Council (RSAC) and the Entertainment Software Ratings Board (ESRB). While neither is particularly helpful, the RSAC appears to do a better job providing content information.

The next time you're at the store, spend a few minutes scanning the covers of today's video games. Look for a black and white seal typically on the lower front of the package. The ESRB uses a system of K-A (appropriate for kids to adults); K-A 6+ (6-year-olds through adults); T–13+ (teenagers 13 and older); and M–17+ (suitable for youth 17+ to adult). From time to time, I found this code supplemented with a statement such as "Animated violence, blood and gore."

By contrast, the RSAC uses the thermometer approach where the level of violence, language, or nudity/sex categories are displayed in miniature, 4-stage thermometers. Further, they define what the level of explicitness represents. Take, for example, the language thermometer. A game might be rated level-2 for mild expletives, or level-3 for profanity.

One popular game called "Duke Nuken" received the highest RSAC violence level for "wanton and gratuitous violence," plus a lower level rating for "revealing attire" and "mild expletives." Another game entitled "Quake" has a level-3 violence and a level-2 language rating.

But problems persist. As informative as both rating systems attempt to be, it's *not* safe to assume their standard is remotely similar to your standard. Another concern is the inconsistent way retailing packages are labeled. I found the hit game "Diablo" rated M−17+. But the additional modules that are available to expand the game were all unrated.

Likewise, there are numerous companies who play by their own rules and refuse to adhere to one of these 2 rating systems. I came across a game with a man pictured on the cover hanging to death. Its lame warning read: "This game contains adult subject matter. Parental guidance is suggested." Really, now. Then there are the makers of "Phantasmagoria" who sport a M−17+ on the package cover, but on the back they suggest a younger age of 13.

CHILD'S PLAY

As you search for appropriate video games (either for the computer or TV-based play), the first step is to always check for a rating. Keep in mind there are a host of wonderful games that can be used to stimulate problem solving, improve a young person's mental math, teach a musical instrument, and even motivate the learning of a new language.

For those interested in sheer entertainment, select games that don't rely upon shock value. From helicopter rescues, sub warfare, dogfights in the sky, to racing cars or chasing the chess championship, a game doesn't need to be deviant to be fun. Avoid games that dwell on the themes of witchcraft, battling evil spirits, or dismembering foes.

And finally, there are 3 factors to keep in mind:

Attitude Adjustment

If you permit the usage of video games, remember our concern is broader than just the issue of violence, language, or scantily-clad vixens. Keep your eyes open to any tendencies of a youngster toward becoming withdrawn, more fearful, less trusting, quick tempered, or nervous. If such symptoms surface, suspend play for a season.

Balance

Even with the host of good video games on the market, there's nothing like real-life experiences, chores, and youth group involvement to help developing young people avoid becoming socially retarded. Make sure they have an abundance of contact with the real world and real people.

Time Management

As the saying goes, even too much of a good thing can spell trouble. Even after building a positive video game library, consider limiting game play to an hour a day.

VIRTUAL REALITY

While we've focused on various forms of video games, their use, and their ratings, I'd be remiss if I didn't touch on what's around the corner: virtual reality. Here, individuals don't play the game—they're *in* the game. Utilizing a helmet-like apparatus, the player moves within a field-of-play that he or she sees through a special pair of glasses. The sensations produced are akin to reality.

At present, there are no genuine home versions of virtual reality games (VRGs). But those who predict such things estimate by the year 2000 VRGs may be as commonplace as yesteryear's Gameboy. My prediction is that those in the porn industry will be among the first to exploit this technology. The notion of a virtual sexual experience is just too tempting to bypass . . . and one I pray society will forgo.

Meanwhile, you have your work cut out for you with th choices at hand!

The Web We Weave

Safe Surfing for Young Cybernauts

We're more likely to destroy ourselves than we ever were. We're a technological world, and we're blind to the terrible toll that technology is exacting all around us.

WILLIAM SHATNER[1]

Today, I need your undivided attention.
If you are distracted by a crying baby, an unruly child, or something as simple as too much stress, consider putting the book down. I'm completely serious. Plan on coming back to it when you are able to be fully focused. If that sounds a bit melodramatic, accept my apologies. However, that doesn't change the intensity and importance of today's topic: pornography and predators on the World Wide Web—and what you must do to protect your family.

At the outset, allow me to underline the fact that the Web can be a fantastic tool for learning, growth, recreation, and study. As a professional writer, I find that the Internet places incredible resources at my fingertips. Adults benefit from on-line news services, stock trades, and travel arrangements. Even children can receive excellent assistance with their homework, visit the world's museums, and even have their poetry published. On those levels I'm a big fan.

But let me be clear: Technology, no matter how wonderful, must have safeguards which protect the most vulnerable members of this global community. As of this writing, those safeguards do not exist, which prompts a heated debate between responsible citizens and Internet purists. I, for one, refuse to sacrifice innocence on the altar of arrogant free speech activists. Nor do I accept the notion propounded by prominent leaders that the inevitable exposure to pornographic images is the risk we take and the price we are required to pay for this new marvel.

It's possible you're thinking, "Whoa, Bob. You're way ahead of me. The World Wide What? Predators prowling where? Internet pornography? Certainly not in my home! Is this really an issue?" Yes. If you've seen (as I've witnessed) children addicted to hard-core pornography, children who have been abducted through contact made on the Internet, or marriages that have taken a beating due to a new on-line relationship, you realize something must be done. So permit me to provide a layperson's response to your questions, along with practical steps you can take to guard your family from the invasion of cyberspace.

CAUGHT IN THE WEB WORDING

Are you tangled up in all of this talk about the Web? Then let's begin by straightening out the concept. An easy way to do that is to simply picture the houses around your neighborhood. It's a safe assumption that every household has at least one telephone as well as a street address. Using a phone book, you're able to locate both a phone and street number of a neighbor. Do you desire to visit or speak with an individual across town? No problem. Just call or stop by using the information provided in the phone directory.

To take this example one step further, not everyone in a given neighborhood is an upstanding citizen. While the majority of friends you might contact or places you might visit are responsible, there are those places that house unsavory—even dangerous—characters. That's a crude picture of how the World Wide Web works.

Essentially, people and businesses from around the globe are connected together into a "virtual neighborhood." Instead of using streets, participants are linked via modem-equipped computers. Each member of this community has an electronic address (also known as a site) where you can send mail, referred to as e-mail. And, much like your community, while the majority are trustworthy individuals, there are those who exist to profit from the sale of the most vile forms of human degradation—hard-core pornography.

And unlike the real world, which uses the telephone for purposes of conversation, devices such as "chat rooms" (which is the modern-day equivalent of a telephone party line) and instant messages (live, interactive typing of a dialogue between two people) are utilized. Down the road this somewhat stunted communication style promises to include voice and video options.

Until then, serious flaws exist. For instance, it is a common practice to use a fictitious name when setting up an electronic address. I could call myself "Joey," "Michael," or even "Sally," "Mary" or "Karen." Further, without the aid of a visual image, I can make up how old I am, what I look like, what I do for a living—even whether I'm married or single. The tragedy is that this lack of verification enables pedophiles to pose as kids. They can "play" in the chat rooms reserved for legitimate children—a favorite place to lure unsuspecting youngsters into meeting in real life.

Likewise, lonely married individuals can fake their marital status as they "meet" new friends in this electronic environment. How harmful could that be? It was sad to learn of a widely-popular mass market author who reportedly dumped his wife of 17 years in favor of a woman he met in cyberspace. I'd say that's serious business.

So why is this important to you and your family?

For several reasons: (1) Our world is rapidly relying upon Web communication technology; (2) most parents are ill-equipped to recognize and prevent the dangers that lurk in the Web; and, (3) computer literate children are surfing the Internet with little or no parental guidance.

Even if you don't own a computer armed with a modem, your young people can become exposed to pornographic pictures at a number of local libraries, schools, or a friend's home where parental supervision is minimal. What can you do? I thought you'd never ask!

PROGRAMMED TO PROTECT

In the spring of 1997, a leading consumer watchdog organization rated 5 so-called blocking software programs. They found the most popular programs were CyberPatrol, Net Nanny, Cybersitter, SurfWatch, and Internet Explorer. Each was created to serve as a protective defense against access to pornographic sites. Some offer the added feature of customized parental controls, which can prevent the disclosure of personal information by a child. Information such as name, address, phone, credit-card data—even profanity can be regulated. Sounds good, right?

Unfortunately, the testing organization concluded that *none* of these safeguard software packages was completely effective. The reason? For one, some programs are not compatible with all computers. It's best to check compatibility before purchasing.

In addition, the Web literally changes and expands by the hour. Because people and companies are moving into this virtual community at such an incredible pace, it's understandable that no software can offer a complete safeguard.

That's where you come in.

Explain the Dangers

You've probably discussed the issue of talking to strangers with your children. Have a similar conversation about people unknown to them on the Internet. Explain to your kids they're never to give any personal information (including a phone number) to anyone they meet on the Web. Likewise, tell your little cybernaut he or she is not permitted to download a file (which is like receiving mail at home from a complete stranger). It may contain pornography or even a computer virus.

Use the Find Feature

Your system should have a function called "FIND." This valuable program permits you to search all hard drives for a particular file or word. Picture files typically bear one of the following suffixes: .gif, .sit, .jpg, .zip, .tif. Type those letters into the FIND program. It will alert you if images exist. Then open those files to see if they're a harmless image or evidence that someone has been dabbling in porn. Keep in mind, many porn sites provide free, unedited samples. Typically, these files are located in a folder called "Downloads."

Review the Browser

Another place to look for an indication of inappropriate Web surfing (which is like channel surfing on your TV) is the browser folder. It contains an extensive collection of files (some are text, others are pictures) the computer uses as an individual visits various Web sites. Many of these items add functionality to the Internet. Others are evidence of pornographic participation.

As I prepared my research for this chapter, something incredibly unexpected occurred. I had set the parental controls on my America On-line account to "teenager," which is supposed to prevent access to "adult" locations on the Web. I wanted to see if I could circumvent the system. In the process, I learned that AOL did a decent job of blocking most porn locations.

However, AOL offered ZERO blocking to a listing of porn sites. In fact, it provided a list of more than 100,000 places to find hard-core pornography on the Web. Each site has a descriptive summary. Even with the teen controls operative, I was able to read about acts of sodomy, group sex, orgies, pornographic descriptions of body parts, and a host of obscene language.

As wretched as that is, AOL also displayed the Internet or Web address, which I could copy down and access on a friend's unblocked computer or on an unblocked computer at a public library. Making my notes, I signed off the Internet saddened at this awful abuse of such a wonderful resource.

Here's the twist. The next day as I went to resume my research, I discovered that AOL had canceled my account. A representative claimed that someone had used my screen name to solicit a child for private information! I freaked out. First of all, we weren't home when the incident occurred. Secondly, it frightened me that there are computer hackers who can tap into my account and use it for evil.

Perhaps that wake-up call will help you understand why I began the chapter as I did. It might even motivate you to turn back to the questions I raised in Day 10 on music. You could adapt that line of inquiry with the Internet in mind. Why? To help your teens *want* to avoid the trashy online influences. With your guidance, the World Wide Web has so much to offer. Without it, it's a potentially dangerous playground for your young people.

Avoiding Ad-nausea

Understanding the Art of Ad Manipulation

There is no question but that someone is speaking into your mind and wants you to do something. First, keep watching. Second, carry the images around in your head. Third, buy something. Fourth, tune in tomorrow.

JERRY MANDER[1]

What do you think is the reason television exists? If you answered "to provide people with a source of interesting programming," you'd be only partially correct. The leading purpose is to attract and satisfy the *advertisers*—not you. Surprised? Of course, what ultimately encourages the muckety-mucks on Madison Avenue to invest in television is to find you sitting comfortably before the tube for extended periods of time. So you and I do serve a purpose!

If you have your doubts that TV exists primarily as a medium for advertisers, try this tonight. Count the number of minutes of commercial messages during one regular hour of prime time. The reason it needs to be a "regular" hour is that oftentimes the advertising base is mini-mized during certain special features or television epics.

Are you interested in a forecast? I predict that you'll find a full 20 minutes out of the hour is dedicated to advertising. As you tally up the ad time, calculate anything that is not specifi-cally the program you chose to watch. Station promos, news briefs, and self-promotions get lumped into the advertising cat-egory. Why? Because they essentially serve as an ad for coming attractions. Even the news briefs are placed there as a teaser for you to watch the 10 o'clock evening report.

Then, consider this question: If TV does not exist for the sake of the advertisers, why is 33% of every hour (that's 1 out of every 3 minutes) dedicated to ad space?

As an interesting parallel, a majority of magazines contain upwards of 35–55% advertising. In addition to counting the number of minutes on television dedicated to ad space, you might also bring a favorite magazine to the table and count all the pages that have ads. Compare that figure to the total num-ber of magazine pages for your percentage.

Given the fact that we are literally surrounded by demands to buy something, today our goal is to (1) understand how most advertisements work, and (2) prepare ourselves to be discern-ing in this aspect of the media culture.

SUPPLIES ARE LIMITED!

We've documented that ad messages dominate the entertain-ment scene. But how do they compel us to buy? Stay tuned while we look at 3 techniques. First, for an ad to be effective, it must have a *strategy of persuasion*. Whether a TV, radio, or print ad, this strategy is likely to appeal to our *feelings, wants,* or *fears.* Why? Advertisers know that feelings bypass the analytical process. You and I are discouraged from pondering the deeper implications of what we see promoted.

Take, for example, a simple product such as French fries. If an ad for fries appealed to our logic, we'd never eat them. Logically speaking, fries are a health threat. The fat and sodium content clogs arteries and raises blood pressure. Simply put, fries cannot be sold using a logical appeal. But if an advertiser pictured warm, radiant faces of happy children sharing a fry with their loving parent—now, that's a different story! Who wouldn't be attracted to the good feelings it evokes?

A second technique used by the advertising community is to *heighten expectations*. How? By creating an illusion of the benefits of product X. Like sheep to the slaughter, we're lured into parting with our hard earned cash-chasing the dream we think exists on the other end of the toll-free number.

Need proof? Then take a peek into the millions of garages and attics that now house a rusting Ab-roller gadget. Well-tanned hard-bodied sales models assured us "with just 5 minutes a day" we can have "the Abs you've always dreamed of." All that was necessary was $129 in "4 easy payments." After hundreds of millions of dollars were spent by consumers, an independent testing organization found such apparatuses added little benefit over a basic stomach crunch.

A final ad strategy we need to address is what I'll call *downplay the negative*. When Burger King pushes its 99¢ Whopper, that's a real deal. Or is it? From a cash perspective, it's a true value. But in terms of health—forget it. You'll never find BK providing the fat content of a burger in their ads.

Even Colonel Sanders is chicken. I recall reading in a trade journal why Kentucky Fried Chicken changed its name to the friendlier handle KFC. During the fat-conscience eighties, the use of the word "fried" in your corporate name was sure to spell indigestion for the bottom line. In a move to downplay the negative, they opted for their initials.

Likewise, cigarette companies never discuss the negative consequences and severe risks of smoking—except what they've been required by law to do! A case in point is Wayne McLaren, the original Marlboro Man. Tragically, in 1992, Wayne died of—surprise!—cancer. He was a mere 51 years of age. Even after his death, Marlboro used his likeness when promoting their products. If you think they ran an ad "in loving memory of Wayne McLaren" after he passed away, guess again.

BUT WAIT, THERE'S MORE

Today I'd like for you to casually bring up this subject of advertising at dinner. With the older children, use either a TV or print ad. Invite them to discover *the strategy of persuasion* and how the advertisement might be used to *heighten expectations*. And if the kids are really sharp, see if they can identify how the advertiser *downplays the negative* aspects.

You'll be surprised at how this process will sharpen their discernment skills regarding future ad messages. The obvious benefit is when they begin to *evaluate* what's being sold instead of acting on their feelings. Come to think of it, that's something you and I could benefit from, too.

Meet the Press

Your Bias Is Showing

In journalism there has always been a tension between getting it first and getting it right.

ELLEN GOODMAN,
BOSTON GLOBE COLUMNIST[1]

Take this quick quiz. What do these people have in common: Rodney King, JonBenet Ramsey, O. J. Simpson, Ted Bundy, Ennis Cosby, David Koresh, the unibomber, Timothy McVeigh, and Paula Jones? Give up? For better or worse, each individual dominated the national news scene for a season. It's safe to say all of them became virtually a household name. Given the powerful place today's news media holds in shaping national events and public opinion, I'd like to spend a few moments with you examining media bias.

Before you tune out, let me ask a few questions. For starters, how do you stay informed of national and local news? Do you receive a newspaper? Is the evening news watched in your home? Does CNN babble away portions of your day? Do you have a news-talk radio station programmed into the memory of your car radio? Further, do you think today's media reflects a bias contrary to the values of your family?

If you answered yes to any of these questions, it's imperative to discover how to prevent your family from being manipulated by the mainstream media. Which is precisely our goal today.

TRUTH MANIPULATORS

Have you ever thought about the fact that when we watch the evening news, read a newspaper, or listen to radio news, we voluntarily give the control of our senses over to the producers of what we're reading or watching? We can learn only what they elect for us to know. Their ideals, values, priorities—yes, their world-life view dominates the story. Their what? A world-life view is roughly along the lines of a creed—it defines what one believes to be right and true.

Why is this important?

Because the value system of the reporter or newscaster determines the slant—or bias—that a story will ultimately reflect. This process is especially dangerous when the slant masquerades behind the pretense of "news." For example, if journalists are personally sympathetic to the issue of homosexual marriages, they'll be inclined to produce a story that *leads the viewer* to share in that perspective. If we're not discerning, we can become persuaded to alter our belief system on "alternative lifestyles."

How can we best prepare our young people to be properly equipped in this area? Meet the press. Discover how the news is actually created. You can do that by making an opportunity to tour a local television station or newspaper headquarters. While you're there, drop by their news center.

JUST THE FACTS, MA'AM

I'll never forget the impression made by my initial visit. As I entered the news room of a Pittsburgh-based studio, I noted a dry-erase board with two columns on it. The left side listed a number of "hot" local stories for the evening news: a convenience store murder, a bank robbery, a porn shop protest, a fire, and so on.

In the right column corresponding with the stories were numbers, such as :21, :17, :35, and the like. Turning to the program director, I asked what the numbers signified. He informed me this was their Master Story Planner and the numbers represented the length of each story in *seconds*.

Consider with me the implication of that for our daily TV news diet. It means Joe Newscaster has typically between 17 and 30 seconds to communicate what happened, both sides of the story, any quotable sound bites, and an event summary (also known as the wrap-up). While I was still recovering from that surprising revelation, the news director explained their "in-depth" story was typically anything longer than 30 seconds, but rarely more than 90.

My first lesson: due to short viewer attention spans the news is shallow and, as such, tends to rely upon the sensational. Think about it. If you had to tell your spouse that you wrecked the car, how it happened, who was at fault, if there were injuries, and what it will cost to repair the damaged vehicle— could you do it in 18 seconds? With that kind of time pressure, I know I'd be forced to choose my words carefully. There's simply no room for fluff.

After you reported the news to your spouse about the crackup, wouldn't it be likely that he or she would have a few questions of his or her own? I'm confident that no matter how hard you may have worked to weigh your words carefully, 18

seconds is simply an inadequate amount of time to fully understand anything of substance.

Yet isn't that the way we receive the news every evening?
We're provided with a breaking story and, in most instances, the
entire report is less than half a minute. So why do we keep tun-
ing in to such shallowness? On the surface, perhaps it's because
we feel "in touch" and somehow connected to the global community. We're magically transported to the scene where it all
happened, so we have a false feeling of "being there."

But between the hasty pace of news and our willingness to
listen and not question, it's easy for journalists to place their
own "spin" (bias) on a story. And that's where we can run into
trouble. To make my point, here's an exercise you can use with
your older young people.

Below is a list of words that are commonly used in reports
dealing with the issue of abortion. Explain to your kids that
you'd like for them to write a fictitious news story about an
abortion clinic protest. Here are the facts they can use: (1) A
local doctor was performing abortions in the third trimester; (2)
100 people staged a protest; and, (3) no arrests were made.

Now, using key words from the list provided, have them write
a news account of the event representing opposite sides of the
issue. Assign one person to take a pro-life vantage point and
another to take a pro-abortion view. If they do their job cor-
rectly, they'll select words that best suit their outlook. Oh, and
just for fun, restrict their final report to something that can be
read in 18 seconds.

After working through this process, they'll be in a better position to more clearly discern a newscaster's bias when reporting
a story. A follow-up re-enforcement of this lesson would be to
find and bring a newspaper story to the dinner table. Using a
yellow highlighter, have the family indicate any words or sound
bites they feel betray the bias or world-life view of the writer.

Abortion Story Key Words

Pro-life	Trimester
Anti-choice	Clinic
Fetus	Right to choose
Unborn child	Right to life
Baby	Choose Life
Tissue	Abortion provider
Abortion	"Abortuary"
Murder	Prayerful
Terminate	Activist
Irate	Alarmist
Blocked	Protesters
Peaceful	Vigil
Alternatives	Life chain
Adoption	Demonstrators
Preborn	Picket
Pregnancy	Partial birth abortion
Term	Post-abortion syndrome

Let me offer just a few other techniques to employ when detecting media bias in a news story or article.

- In an abortion story whom did the journalist choose to quote? If the president of the National Organization of Women was selected instead of the president of the National Right to Life, that would denote bias. Watch for "an unnamed source" or "key sources." There is no way to verify the accuracy of such information.
- Notice the amount of time (in TV and radio news) or the number of paragraphs devoted to presenting one side of a story over another. Bias often determines what side gets heard—and for how long.
- You'll find that many journalists will do a decent job presenting both sides of a story. Then they insert the word

"But" in their wrap-up. That often signals the reporter's chosen slant is about to follow. Beware!

Have your kids spot these tactics during a newscast. When it's time for the commercial break, mute the sound and discuss what they found. Besides being a fun exercise, this activity provides children with a powerful tool to comprehend and prevent media mind manipulation in the days ahead.

DAY 21

Activist, Flasher, or Lifer?

Keeping an Eye on the Long Haul

This country will never again be healthy if we don't have the courage to confront the spiritual and cultural and moral deficit that is an even greater threat to our future than the economic deficit.

NEWT GINGRICH[1]

Can you believe we've worked for three weeks already on making better entertainment choices for your home? Looking back, how did you do? Did your family embrace the new ideas we discussed? If so, congratulations. You're on your way. You've set the stage for a lifetime of critical thinking for your clan. And you've imparted something to your precious ones that few parents nurture: a discerning spirit.

On the other hand, if you didn't witness sweeping changes in the family's entertainment diet, don't let that depress you. Were there times when you had the right intentions but the words or your approach didn't come out right? If so, don't be discouraged. Let me assure you, you're not alone. In fact, leading American corporations with huge marketing departments run into the same communication difficulties when reaching a new audience.

For example, when Coca-Cola was introduced to the Chinese, they rendered it as "Ke-kou-ke-la." What they didn't discover until too late was that phrase is literally translated, "Bite the wax tadpole." Depending on the dialect, it could also mean "Female horse stuffed with wax." Too bad for Coke—they had thousands of signs painted with that slogan. Talk about miscommunication. Oh, after more careful research they finally settled on a loose phonetic equivalent with "ko-kou-ko-le" which means, "Happiness in the mouth."

Pepsi's pop sales were flat in Taiwan when they first introduced their "Come alive with the Pepsi Generation." Why? The translation yielded, "Pepsi will bring your ancestors back from the dead." Ford Motor Company drove into trouble with their Pinto sales in Brazil. Evidently, Pinto just happens to be Brazilian slang for "tiny male genitals." Not until Ford pried Pinto nameplates off their cars and replaced them with Corcel (translated "horse") did sales get a running start.

DROP BACK AND PUNT

Look at it this way. If major players like Coke, Pepsi, and Ford with their millions of dollars and thousands of employees fumbled around, it's possible that you may need to go back to the drawing board on a few of the concepts we've considered these last 20 days. That's okay. There's nothing wrong with regrouping and approaching the family again.

To that end, maybe spend a few moments today in quiet reflection. In which aspects of your family's entertainment diet did you witness the most cooperation—and the highest level of resistance—to change? What might you do differently in the future?

There's a reason why this analysis is so vital. If you can't tell by now, our 21 days together is bigger than simply making better personal entertainment choices. At the heart of our conversation is the issue of becoming the kingdom player God desires us to be instead of becoming spiritually neutralized. And it's about maturing into a godly individual who has a deep, inner cistern of wisdom from which to drink during difficult times.

I believe the primary negative consequence of participation in today's entertainment is the *displacement of time* for more important activities. The longer the TV is on and the more mindless movies we watch, the less time there is for quiet reflection, enriching real-life interaction—even our personal devotions suffer. Junior may have the top score on the video game, but how's he rank in his understanding of God's Word? And, if you and I don't set the right example, how will our children develop a hunger for the Lord?

The psalmist beautifully captured the essence of what we're talking about when he sang, "Oh, how I love your law! I meditate on it all day long. Your commands make me wiser than my enemies, for they are ever with me. I have more insight than all my teachers, for I meditate on your statutes" (Ps. 119:97–99). I pray that God will use my efforts to effect that kind of yearning in the hearts of each member of my family. How about you?

IT'S A MARATHON, NOT A SPRINT

As your coach, I believe a final challenge is in order. There's a reason you've read this far. Based upon my years of experience, you are likely one of 3 kinds of personality types: an activist, a flasher, or a lifer. I'd like for you to reflect upon the differences between them. As we do, consider which one best describes you:

The Activist

Being an activist can be a good thing. But in this instance, I'm referring to the woman who takes this message to an unhealthy extreme. Anywhere she goes, the activist carries with her reams of papers documenting some aspect of trash on TV or radio. This individual takes an almost crusade-like approach. Bashing entertainment has become a purpose for living. Frankly, she's not much fun to be around—or live with!

The Flasher

No, I'm not referring to the guy who exposes himself in an indecent manner. This individual is driven by an event that sparks a sudden response. It might be a lewd commercial during a family TV show, a crude billboard along the highway, or nasty music pulsating by the pool side. Whatever the cause, he panics and calls every pro-family organization in the phone book. The flasher gets all worked up and demands immediate action. But his enthusiasm isn't extended beyond a few days. Like a flash in the pan, he's gone before long ... until something triggers him again.

The Lifer

The best word to describe lifers is *steadiness*. These unwavering individuals understand that humankind has an evil heart. They're not surprised when Hollywood works overtime to insult and attack their families' values. In contrast to flashers, lifers are committed to the long haul. They see discernment as a way of life. And, unlike activists, lifers exhibit balance. They know when to speak ... and when to release.

How about you? Which adjective best describes your approach? I see myself as a lifer. If there comes a day when I am no longer engaged in the full-time study of popular culture, and if I were to stop writing and speaking on this subject, I'd still work within my family to make the best possible entertainment choices. It's not a job, it's a way of life. You might say it's in my blood. I can't get away from it—nor do I ever desire to! Why?

The benefits to my family and me are too great.

The payoff for us is priceless.

And the Lord, through our proper choices, is honored.

OTHER RESOURCES
from Bob DeMoss

Books:

- *Learn to Discern* (Zondervan), 1997.
- *Sex & the Single Person* (Zondervan), 1995.

Videos:

- *Learn to Discern: Help for a Generation at Risk* (Entertainment Today). Available in both Christian and secular editions. For details, write the address below.

Seminars:

- *Learn to Discern*: a multi-media examination of music, media, and pop culture, designed for either teen or adult audiences.
- *Hope for the Single Heart*: a program designed to help singles deal with issues of intimacy and sexuality.

For booking information, write:
Bob DeMoss
Entertainment Today, Inc.
Box 121,228
Nashville, TN 37212.

NOTES

DAY 1: Breakfast of Champions?

1. Rosalie Maggio, *Quotations by Women* (Boston: Beacon Press, 1996), 685.

DAY 2: Inclined Recliner

1. Rosalie Maggio, *Quotations by Women* (Boston: Beacon Press, 1996), 685.

DAY 3: When Pay TV Pays Off

1. Dr. Laurence J. Peter, *Peter's Quotations* (New York: Quill, 1977), 325.

DAY 4: Door Prizes, Jackpots, and Gifts Galore!

1. Dr. Laurence J. Peter, *Peter's Quotations* (New York: Quill, 1977), 77.

DAY 5: Two Ways to Watch What You Watch

1. Ashton Applewhite, William R. Evans III, Andrew Frothingham, *And I Quote* (New York: St. Martin's Press, 1992), 314.

2. Frank Rich, in an editorial, *The New York Times*, December 18, 1996.

DAY 6: Your Secret Weapon

1. Rosalie Maggio, *Quotations by Women* (Boston: Beacon Press, 1996), 543.

DAY 7: Setting Standards When Settings Aren't Standard

1. Susan Sarandon, *TV Guide*, 4/13/96.

DAY 8: Making Beautiful Music

1. Trent Reznor, *RollingStone*, 3/6/97.

DAY 9: Wise Shoppers Avoid Wise Mouths

1. Timothy White, *Billboard*, 6/29/96.
2. Not his real name.

DAY 10: Lyrical Analysis for Amateurs

1. John Leo, Viewpoints column, *Dallas Morning News*, 12/31/96.

DAY 11: Feedback & Faithful Fathering

1. Chris Carter, *Rolling Stone*, 2/20/97.

DAY 12: A Little Sound Advice

1. Joe Wheeler, *Remote Controlled* (Hagerstown, MD: Review & Herald Publishing Association, 1993), 19.
2. Marilyn Manson bandmate Twiggy, *RollingStone*, 1/23/97.
3. A partial list includes Genesis, YES, Chicago, Eric Clapton, Motley Crue, AC/DC, Metallica, Def Leppard, Alice Cooper, Black Sabbath, Van Halen, Crosby, Stills, Nash and Young, Heart, Megadeth, Ozzy Osbourne, Kansas, ZZ Top, Iron Maiden, Janet Jackson, Rolling Stones, Chuck Berry, and, yes, even Michael Jackson. This list doesn't include literally hundreds of Christian concerts.

DAY 13: It's Showtime!

1. Rosalie Maggio, *Quotations by Women* (Boston: Beacon Press, 1996), 148.

DAY 15: Cinema or "Sin-ema"

1. Rosalie Maggio, *Quotations by Women* (Boston: Beacon Press, 1996), 685.
2. I also left part way through the Oscar-winning best picture of 1996 *The English Patient*. In that case, it was a combination of boredom and offense at the topic of adultery.
3. Joe Wheeler, *Remote Controlled* (Hagerstown, MD: Review and Herald Publishing, 1993), 19.

DAY 16: Magazine Madness

1. Dr. Laurence J. Peter, *Peter's Quotations* (New York: Quill, 1977), 325.

2. *Teen*, February, 1997.

DAY 17: Virtuous Video Veggies

1. Bob Strauss, *Entertainment Weekly*, Fall Double Issue, 1996.

DAY 18: The Web We Weave

1. William Shatner, *The Tennessean*, 9/4/96.

DAY 19: Avoiding Ad-nausea

1. Jerry Mander, *Four Arguments for the* Elimination *of Television* (New York: Morrow Quill Paperbacks, 1978), 169.

DAY 20: Meet the Press

1. Rosalie Maggio, *Quotations by Women* (Boston: Beacon Press, 1996), 370.

DAY 21: Activist, Flasher, or Lifer?

1. Newt Gingrich, *WORLD*, 12/7/96.

Look for all eight books in the 21 Days Series

The **21 Days Series** is perfect for anyone wanting to affect positive changes in their life. Studies have shown that virtually any habit can be established in a 21-day period. That's the idea behind the **21 Days Series**. If you are willing to concentrate on one important habit, using a day-by-day plan for change, then you can make positive, lasting improvements in your life.

In *21 Days to Enjoying Your Bible*, youth leader and author Todd Temple shows you why the Bible is so fascinating, how to navigate its pages, how it is organized, and what personal, practical help the Bible offers. Softcover 0-310-21745-8

In *21 Days to Eating Better*, Gregory Jantz, who is founder and executive director of The Center for Counseling and Health Resources, uses proven strategies to teach you how to replace negative eating habits with energizing, healthy ways to feed and nurture not only the body but also your mind and soul.
Softcover 0-310-21747-4

21 Days to a Thrifty Lifestyle by Mike Yorkey is all about spending money wisely, revealing practical ways to track expenses, how to save money, how to avoid being ripped off, and even includes plans for retirement, health care, and much more.
Softcover 0-310-21752-0

21 Days to Better Family Entertainment by youth culture expert Bob DeMoss supplies sensible advice to help families regain control of TV, music, movies, the Internet, and other forms of home entertainment. Here's a creative, realistic approach to trading media overload for a better family life. Softcover 0-310-21746-6

Available in April 1998:

In *21 Days to a Better Quiet Time with God*, author Timothy Jones shows readers how taking just a few minutes from their day to share with God can enrich their lives immensely.
Softcover 0-310-21749-0

In *21 Days to Better Fitness*, leading health and fitness author Maggie Greenwood-Robinson offers readers a simple, day-by-day strategy for improving their fitness and health.
Softcover 0-310-21750-4

21 Days to Helping Your Child Learn by Cheri Fuller is a short course in teaching kids the joys of thinking creatively and learning naturally.
Softcover 0-310-21748-2

21 Days to Financial Freedom features a simple and practical financial plan that anyone can use, from the series' editor Dan Benson.
Softcover 0-310-21751-2

ZondervanPublishingHouse
Grand Rapids, Michigan
http://www.zondervan.com

We want to hear from you. Please send your comments about
this book to us in care of the address below. Thank you.

ZondervanPublishingHouse
Grand Rapids, Michigan 49530
http://www.zondervan.com